Patient Care Technician
Certification Exam Review Questions

Vol 1

PCT Test Prep

Jane John-Nwankwo CPT, RN, MSN, PHN

Patient Care Technician Exam Certification Review Questions: PCT Test Prep

ISBN-13: 978-1482783346
ISBN-10: 1482783347

Printed in the United States of America.

Dedication

Dedicated to my mother, Patricia Onwere who gave me all the love I needed in my childhood

OTHER TITLES FROM THE SAME AUTHOR:

1. Director of Staff Development: The Nurse Educator

2. Crisis Prevention & Intervention in Healthcare: Management of Assaultive Behavior

3. CNA Exam Prep: Nurse Assistant Practice Test Questions. Vol. One

4. CNA Exam Prep: Nurse Assistant Practice Test Questions. Vol Two

5. IV Therapy & Blood Withdrawal Review Questions

6. Medical Assistant Test Preparation

7. EKG Test Prep

8. Phlebotomy Test Prep

9. The Home Health Aide Textbook

10. How to make a million in nursing

Order these books now at www.bestamericanhealthed.com/resources.html
Or call 951 637 8332 for bulk purchases

TABLE OF CONTENTS

Introduction

Patient Care Technicians can simply be said to be a combination of nurse assistants and medical assistants because they perform the duties of nurse assistants as well as the duties of medical assistants. They work under the supervision of nursing or medical staff to provide basic patient care which may include the following:

– recording vital signs, height, weight, input output, collect and test specimens, report and record patient conditions and patient treatments.

-Helping patients with nutritional needs; check and deliver food trays, assist with feeding the patient when necessary, and refilling water and ice.

-Assist patients with their mobility ;turning and positioning, do range of motion exercises, transferring patients to and from wheelchair, assist with ambulation.

To become a patient care technician specialized training is required.

Many students use the PCT training and knowledge as a stepping stone to further their medical careers and become Licensed Vocational Nurses or Registered Nurses.

Clinical job duties of the Patient Care Assistant may include: Discontinuation of catheters, cleaning and irrigating lacerations, answering phones, locating equipment and the transport of non Critical Patients as well as assist with critical patients, foley catheters discontinuation, dressing changes, feeding patients, assisting with comfort measures / safety Measures, attending to the mental health patients and escorting patients to treatment areas, cleaning patient's environment, collecting specimens, clinical documentation, changing sharp boxes and O2; decontamination procedures, setting up and interpreting EKG's, assisting with O2 delivery, cleaning instruments and post-mortem care, preparing charts for admissions, splint assistance, suctioning, helping with patient ambulation, take vital signs and assist with pelvic exams, and perform phlebotomy procedures.

The PCT provides basic nursing care on assigned patients as delegated by the RN ,LVN or LPN and completes other duties as required.

This book is a compilation of more than 800 questions ranging from basic nursing care, EKG, Phlebotomy, career development and professional ethics questions to help patient care technician students challenge their certification exams.

Section One

1. In the Medical Terminology the word **"Half"** has which of the following Prefixes?
   a. Demi
   b. Semi
   c. Hemi
   d. Duo

2. In the Medical Terminology the prefix **"dia-"** means?
   a. Two
   b. Die
   c. Complete
   d. Deficient

3. In the Medical Terminology the prefix **"Hypo-"** means?
   a. Over
   b. Under
   c. More than Normal
   d. Less than Normal

4. In the Medical Terminology the prefix **"Tachy"** means?
   a. Attach
   b. Fast
   c. Slaw
   d. After

5. In the Medical Terminology the prefix **"Auto"** means?
   a. Self
   b. Start
   c. Automatic
   d. Car

6. In the Medical Terminology the prefix **"Retro"** means?
   a. Behind
   b. Before
   c. Old
   d. Reverse

7. In the Medical Terminology the suffix **"-dynia"** means?
   a. Blood Condition
   b. Die
   c. Two
   d. Pain

8. In the Medical Terminology the suffix **"-osis"** means?

a. Inflammation
b. Protein
c. Condition
d. Disease
e.

9. In the Medical Terminology the suffix **"-penia"** means?
    a. Prolong
    b. Pain
    c. Deficiency
    d. Softening

10. In the Medical Terminology the suffix **"-carcino"** means?
    a. Casino
    b. Malignant Tumor
    c. Enlargement
    d. Condition

11. In the Medical Terminology the suffix **"-Malacia"** means?
    a. Softening
    b. Hardening
    c. Enlargement
    d. Deficient

12. What is the meaning of this Medical Abbreviation "NYD"?
    a. Not Yet Diagnosed
    b. Not Your Diagnosis
    c. Not Yet Dead
    d. No your Diet

13. What is the meaning of this Medical Abbreviation "STAT"?
    a. Start
    b. Immediately
    c. Status
    d. Start to Act Today

14. What is the meaning of this Medical Abbreviation "CBC"?
    a. Cell Blood Count
    b. Count Blood Cell
    c. Complete Blood Cell Count
    d. Complete Blood Cell

15. What is the meaning of this Medical Abbreviation "I&O"?
    a. Incision and Output
    b. Inside and Outside
    c. Ion and Out
    d. Intake and Output

16. _____ is the science that studies the function of the human body?
    a. Anatomy
    b. Physiology

c. Nursing
d. Patient Health Care

17. _____ is not a main feature of the Cell?
     a. Membrane
     b. Cytoplasm
     c. Nucleus
     d. Tissue

18. _____ is defined as a group of similar cells performing a specific function?
     a. Membrane
     b. Cytoplasm
     c. Nucleus
     d. Tissue

19. _____ is a type of Muscular Tissue?
     a. Skeletal Striated
     b. Connective tissue
     c. Epithelial tissue
     d. Nervous tissue

20. _____ is a type of Connective Tissue?
     a. Skeletal Striated
     b. Blood
     c. Epithelial tissue
     d. Nervous tissue

21. _____ is a tissue that transmits analyzes and coordinates electrical impulses in response to the changes of the outside environment?
     a. Connective tissue
     b. Epithelial tissue
     c. Nervous tissue
     d. Muscular Tissue

22. _____ is a combination of different tissues, performing complicated and specialized functions.
     a. Membrane
     b. Organ
     c. System
     d. Veins

23. The Medical Terminology for "Back" in the Positional and Directional Term is _____?
     a. Coccygeal
     b. Sacral
     c. Ventral
     d. Dorsal

24. _____ is not an example of intentional Tort
     a. Invasion of privacy
     b. False imprisonment

c. Negligence
d. Assault

25. _____ is a self-understood action of permission not expressed in words or in writing.
    a. Informed Consent
    b. Implied Consent
    c. Right
    d. Authorization

26. _____ are instructions given by individuals specifying what actions should be taken for their health in case they can no longer make proper decision due to illness.
    a. Living Will
    b. Power of Attorney
    c. Patient's Bill of Right
    d. Advanced Health Care Directives

27. _____ is not part of the chain of infection
    a. Susceptible Host
    b. Reservoir Host
    c. Immune System
    d. Agent

28. The Precaution intended to protect all health care providers, patients and their visitors or family members from infectious diseases is called?
    a. Universal Precaution
    b. Standard Precaution
    c. Basic Precaution
    d. Body Fluid Precaution

29. Which of the following is not a Universal Precautions guideline?
    a. Properly report needle stick injuries, splashes, and wound secretion contact and contamination
    b. Never recap a needle
    c. Health care workers with open wounds or lesions, dermatitis or other infectious diseases should not wear gloves before having direct contact with the patients
    d. If gloves are damaged immediately wash your hands and wear a new pair before you continue the procedure

30. The process of identifying the nature and the cause of a disease is called
    a. Prognosis
    b. Diagnosis
    c. Patient's chief complaint
    d. Etiology

31. When recording the patient's medical history the "PQRST" is a good example interview technique. What does the "P" stand for?
    a. Protect
    b. Prolong
    c. Project

d. Provoke

32. The following are part of the 6 Cs of Charting except?
   a. Conciseness
   b. Clarity
   c. Clinical Signs
   d. Client's words

33. The letters S, O, A, and P in SOAP format for progress notes, stand for?
   a. Source, order, assessment, prognosis
   b. Start, objective, align, plan
   c. Subjective, objective, assessment, plan
   d. Selection, objection, appeal, prognosis

34. The symptoms a patient is currently seen for is called?
   a. The prognosis
   b. The diagnosis
   c. The patient record
   d. The chief complaint

35. _____ is the position in which the patient lay on the back with knees flexed and legs are placed above the chest on stirrups and wide apart.
   a. Supine Position
   b. Lithotomy Position
   c. Fowler's Position
   d. Tredelenburg's Position

36. _____ is the position in which the patient is lying supine on a tilted table with the head positioned lower than the legs. It is mostly used to treat hypovolemia
   a. Supine Position
   b. Lithotomy Position
   c. Fowler's Position
   d. Trendelenburg's Position

37. _____ is the position in which the patient is placed on the belly, face down and turned on the side; arms are placed on the side of the body or bent at the elbow and placed under the chest
   a. Prone Position
   b. Lithotomy Position
   c. Proctologic Position:
   d. Trendelenburg's Position

38. _____ is the position in which the patient is bent at the hips at 90 degree angle. The head is placed on the side, and the arms are placed on the side of the body.
   a. Prone Position
   b. Lithotomy Position
   c. Proctologic Position:
   d. Trendelenburg's Position

39. The normal temperature measurement for Axillary is?

a. 98.6 F to 100.6 F (37.0C to 38.1C)
b. 98.6 F (37C)
c. 97.6 F to 99.6 F (36.5C to 37.5C)
d. 96.6 F to 98.6 F (35.9C to 37.0C)

40. The normal temperature measurement for Rectal is?
a. 98.6 F to 100.6 F (37.0C to 38.1C)
b. 98.6 F (37C)
c. 97.6 F to 99.6 F (36.5C to 37.5C)
d. 96.6 F to 98.6 F (35.9C to 37.0C)

41. The normal temperature measurement for Tympanic membrane is?
a. 98.6 F to 100.6 F (37.0C to 38.1C)
b. 98.6 F (37C)
c. 97.6 F to 99.6 F (36.5C to 37.5C)
d. 96.6 F to 98.6 F (35.9C to 37.0C)

42. _____ Is a fever above 104 degrees F (38 degree C)
a. Hyperpyrexia
b. Hypothermia
c. Pyrexia
d. Afebrile

43. _____ Is a body temperature lower than 97 degree F (36 degree C).
a. Hyperpyrexia
b. Hypothermia
c. Pyrexia
d. Afebrile

44. _____ Is the term used when having normal body temperature.
a. Hyperpyrexia
b. Hypothermia
c. Pyrexia
d. Afebrile

45. Fluctuating fever that returns to or below baseline, then rises again is called?
a. Intermittent
b. Remittent
c. Continuous
d. Recurrent

46. Fever that remains fairly constant above the baseline; and does not fluctuate is called?
a. Intermittent
b. Remittent
c. Continuous
d. Recurrent

47. _____ temperature is considered by the majority of the physicians as the most accurate method of temperature measurement
a. Rectal

b. Axillary

c. Tympanic temperature

d. Oral

48. _____ is useful for children and confused patients because of the speed of operation?

 a. Rectal

 b. Axillary

 c. Tympanic temperature

 d. Oral

49. _____ is the least accurate and is taken only when no other temperature site can be used?

 a. Rectal

 b. Axillary

 c. Tympanic temperature

 d. Oral

50. A temporary complete absence of breathing which may be a result of a reduction in the stimuli to the respiratory centers of the brain is called?

 a. Bradypnea

 b. Tachypnea

 c. Apnea

 d. Dyspnea

51. _____ is a decrease in numbers of respirations. This occurs during sleep. It may also be due to certain diseases?

 a. Bradypnea

 b. Tachypnea

 c. Apnea

 d. Dyspnea

52. This is a respiratory rate of greater than 40/min. It is transient in the newborn and maybe caused by the hysteria in the adult.

 a. Bradypnea

 b. Tachypnea

 c. Apnea

 d. Dyspnea

53. Below are abnormalities in the depth of respiration except?

 a. Dyspnea

 b. Orthopnea

 c. Hypoventilation

 d. Tachypnea

54. Difficulty in breathing when lying down is called?

 a. Dyspnea

 b. Orthopnea

 c. Hypoventilation

 d. Tachypnea

55. Slow and shallow respiration is called?
    a. Dyspnea
    b. Orthopnea
    c. Hypoventilation
    d. Tachypnea

56. Pulse rate above 100 beats per minute (bpm) is called?
    a. Tachycardia
    b. Bradycardia
    c. Orthocardia
    d. Cardia

57. Pulse rate below 60 bpm is called?
    a. Tachycardia
    b. Bradycardia
    c. Orthocardia
    d. Cardia

58. The Normal blood pressure for 6-9 years is?
    a. 50/25
    b. 90/60
    c. 95/65
    d. 100/65

59. The Normal blood pressure for Young Adult is?
    a. 95/65
    b. 100/65
    c. 118/76
    d. 120/80

60. The Normal blood pressure for Adult is?
    a. 100/65
    b. 118/76
    c. 120/80
    d. 120/90

61. _____ is a type of card file that summarizes information found in the medical record such as diagnosis, treatments, medications, routine care measures, and special needs.
    a. Progress Notes
    b. Flow sheets
    c. Kardex
    d. Graphic Sheet

62. A sudden drop in blood pressure when the patient changes the position from a lying to sitting or standing up, with signs of dizziness or fainting is called?
    a. Orthostatic Hypotension
    b. Hypertension
    c. Low blood count
    d. Low blood pressure

63. Besides helping and assisting the patient with elimination of urine and feces, the patient care technician should also observe and report the changes in urine except?

a. Quality
b. Odor
c. Texture
d. Sediment

64. A test used to detect the presence of hidden blood in stool is called?
   a. Stool Sample
   b. Fecal occult blood Test
   c. Catch blood stool
   d. Parasite test

65. The following are signs of hypoxia except?
   a. Painful breathing
   b. Fatigue and anxiety
   c. Changes in eye color
   d. Bluish color on fingers and toes

66. Below are some of the respiratory tests used to diagnose respiratory problems or dyspnea except?
   a. Bronchoscopy
   b. Arterial Blood Gases
   c. Thoracocentesis
   d. Fecal occult blood Test

67. Blood clot inside a vessel is called?
   a. Embolus
   b. Wound
   c. Blood vessel cloth
   d. Thrombus

68. The following are the different types of wound drainage except?
   a. Serous
   b. Traumatic
   c. Purulent
   d. Sanguineous

69. _____ is a clear and watery wound drainage that does not contain blood cells?
   a. Serous
   b. Traumatic
   c. Purulent
   d. Sanguineous

70. _____ is a thick greenish, yellowish or brownish wound drainage
   a. Serous
   b. Traumatic
   c. Purulent
   d. Sanguineous

71. _____ receives oxygenated blood returning from the lungs via the right and left pulmonary veins.
   a. Right atrium
   b. Right ventricle
   c. Left atrium
   d. Pulmonary veins

72. _____ receives deoxygenated blood returning to the heart from the body via the superior vena cava
    a. Right atrium
    b. Right ventricle
    c. Left atrium
    d. Pulmonary veins

73. _____ arteries are the only arteries in the body that carry deoxygenated blood.
    a. Pulmonary
    b. Left
    c. Right
    d. Brachiocephalic

74. The heart is a two-sided pump separated by _____
    a. Chamber
    b. Atria
    c. Ventricles
    d. Septum

75. _____ valve is located between the left atrium and the left ventricle
    a. Aortic valve
    b. Mitral valve
    c. Tricuspid valve
    d. Pulmonic valve

76. _____ valve is located between the right atrium and the right ventricle.
    a. Aortic valve
    b. Mitral valve
    c. Tricuspid valve
    d. Pulmonic valve

77. Where is the heart located?
    a. Lungs
    b. Thoracic Cavity
    c. Sternum
    d. Heart Chamber

78. _____ is the outermost layer of the heart
    a. Endocardium
    b. Myocardium
    c. Pericardium
    d. Epicardium

79. _____ is the innermost layer of the heart that forms the lining and folds back onto itself to form the four valves?
    a. Endocardium
    b. Myocardium
    c. Pericardium
    d. Epicardium

80. _____ is the middle and contractile layer of the heart?
   a. Endocardium
   b. Myocardium
   c. Pericardium
   d. Epicardium

81. _____ is a sac in which the heart is contained?
   a. Sternum
   b. Myocardium
   c. Pericardium
   d. Visceral

82. The ability of all cardiac cells to transmit electric stimulus to the other cardiac cells is?
   a. Contractility
   b. Conductivity
   c. Excitability:
   d. Automaticity

83. The ability of the cardiac cells to shorten their length in response to an electrical stimulus is?
   a. Contractility
   b. Conductivity
   c. Excitability
   d. Automaticity

84. _____ is the heart main pacemaker that controls the heart rhythm with a rate of 60 to 100 beats per minute
   a. Inter Nodal Atrial pathways
   b. Sino-Atrial Node
   c. Atrio-Ventricular Node
   d. His Bundle

85. _____ is found at the superior portion of the interventricular septum. It is a highway of the conductive system and can trigger impulses with a rate of 40-60 beats per minute.
   a. Inter Nodal Atrial pathways
   b. Sino-Atrial Node
   c. Atrio-Ventricular Node
   d. Bundle of HIS

86. _____ are the last small branches of the conductive system that connect the ventricular pathways with each muscular fiber?
   a. Purkinje fibers
   b. Bundle branches
   c. AV node
   d. Bundle of His

87. Which of this is not a *Bipolar Standard Lead?*
   a. the left arm is positive and the right arm is negative. (LA – RA)
   b. the left leg is positive and the right arm is negative. (LL – RA)
   c. the left leg is positive and the left arm is negative.(LL – LA)

d. the left arm is positive and the left leg is negative (LA-LL)

Below is a picture of the human heart from questions 88 – 116, label it with the options provided

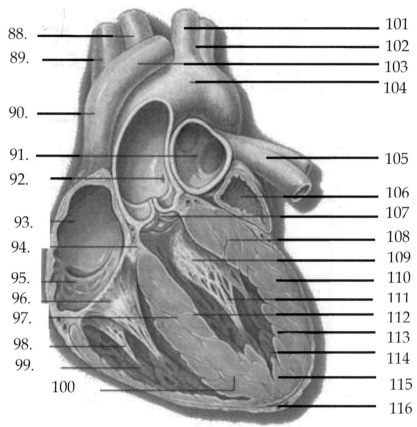

88. _____
89. _____

90. _____

91. _____
92. _____

93. _____
94. _____

95. _____
96. _____
97. _____
98. _____
99. _____

100 _____

_____ 101
_____ 102
_____ 103
_____ 104

_____ 105

_____ 106
_____ 107
_____ 108
_____ 109
_____ 110
_____ 111
_____ 112
_____ 113
_____ 114
_____ 115
_____ 116

Options:

A	B	C	D
Right Brachiocephalic Vein	Left Brachiocephalic Vein	Brachiocephalic Artery	Superior Vena Cava
Pulmonary Trunk	Left Coronary Artery	Right Atrium	Left Pulmonary Artery
Membranous Septum	Tricuspid Valve	Valve of Inferior Vena Cava	Left Atrial Appendage
Inferoseptal Segment of LV	Interventricular Septum	Apical Segment of LV	Chordae Tendineae
Aortic Valve	Apical Septal Segment of LV	Anterolateral Segment of LV	Anterobasal Segment of LV
Apex of Heart	Papillary Muscles	Left Ventricle	Mitral Valve
Aortic Arch	Left Subclavian Artery	Left Common Carotid Artery	None of the Above

117. What is the line between two waveforms called?
    a. Segment

b. Waveform
c. Interval
d. Complex

118. _____ is a wave plus a segment
  a. Segment
  b. Waveform
  c. Interval
  d. Complex

119. Several waveforms is referred to as?
  a. Waveform
  b. Compound
  c. Complex
  d. Multiplex

120. The normal P wave in standard, limb and precordial leads does not exceed_____ in duration
  a. 0.11s
  b. 1.01s
  c. 10.0s
  d. 0.10s

SECTION TWO

1. Mucus from the respiratory system that is expectorated from the mouth is called:

 A. Hemoptysis
 B. Acetone
 C. Melena
 D. Sputum

2. Specimens are collected and tested for the following reasons except:

 A. To prevent disease
 B. To detect disease
 C. For urine control
 D. To treat disease

3. Who orders what specimen to collect and the test needed?

 A. Nurse Aide
 B. Doctor

C. Receptionist
D. Resident's family

4. Which one is a not rule for collecting specimens?

   A. Use only one container for different specimens
   B. Follow the rules of medical asepsis
   C. Label the container
   D. Do not touch the inside of the container or lid.

5. Urine specimens are collected for:
   A. Tarry stool test
   B. Sputum
   C. Blood test
   D. Urine tests

6. Before collecting a urine specimen you need the following information from the nurse except:

   A. The type of specimen needed
   B. What time to collect the specimen?
   C. The marital status of the patient
   D. What special measures are needed?

7. The midstream specimen is also called................?

   A. A sterile voided specimen
   B. A clean-catch urine specimen
   C. Acetone specimen
   D. Ketone specimen

8. All urine voided during a 24 hour period is collected for a _____.

   A. 24 hour urine specimen
   B. 12 hour urine specimen
   C. Double voided specimen
   D. Random specimen

9. Urine tested for ketones are usually collected:

   A. Before breakfast
   B. Thirty minutes after meals and at bed time

C. Thirty minutes before meals and at bed time
D. At midnight

10. Stools are black and tarry if there is bleeding in the:

   A. Intestine
   B. Vagina
   C. Heart
   D. Stomach or upper GI tract.

11. Surgery done by choice to improve the person's life or well-being is called:
   A. Urgent surgery
   B. Emergency surgery
   C. Elective surgery
   D. General surgery

12. Joint replacement surgery and cosmetic surgery are what type of surgery?

   A. General surgery
   B. Elective surgery
   C. Emergency surgery
   D. Urgent surgery

13. The type of surgery that is sudden and unexpected is _____.

   A. Emergency surgery
   B. By-pass surgery
   C. General surgery
   D. Urgent surgery

14. The introduction of fluid into vagina and the immediate return of the fluid is called:

   A. Anesthesia
   B. Thrombus
   C. Embolus
   D. Douche

15. Which is not a common fear and concern of surgical patients?

   A. Pain after surgery
   B. Dying during surgery
   C. Pain during surgery
   D. Comfort surgery

16. Regional anesthesia means:

   A. Generalized loss of consciousness
   B. Loss of feeling or sensation in a particular area of the body
   C. Anesthesia given to a city
   D. Loss of feeling produced by a drug given to a county in a region

17. Preoperative drugs are given to patients about _____ minutes to I hour before surgery.

   A. 45
   B. 10
   C. 5
   D. 15

18. Preoperative drugs are given to the patient for the following reasons except:

   A. To help the person relax an feel drowsy
   B. To stop the person from dying
   C. Reduce respirations, secretions and to prevent aspirations.
   D. To prevent nausea and vomiting

19. A doctor who specializes in giving anesthetics is called:

   A. Podiatrist
   B. Social Worker
   C. Physical therapist
   D. An anesthesiologist

20. As a PCT to help prevent respiratory and circulatory complications after surgery and if the post-surgical orders allow, you should reposition the patient at least:

   A. 96h
   B. q4h
   C. q2h
   D. q3h

21. When preparing a surgical patient bed, you should do the following except:

   A. Use clean Linens
   B. Keep the bed at its lowest position
   C. Lower bed rails

D. Move furniture out of the way for stretcher

22. Elastic stockings are ordered for the people at risk of thrombi. Which patient is not at risk of thrombi?

    A. Pregnant women
    B. Obese patients
    C. Surgical Patients
    D. None of the above

23. Elastic stocking are also called:

    A. Leg wear
    B. Elastic bandages
    C. Anti-embolism stockings
    D. Pressure stockings

24. Preoperatively Mr. Leon is _____.

    A. Given a tube feeding
    B. NPO
    C. Allowed only milk
    D. Allowed only water

CIRCLE T IF THE STATEMENT IS TRUE AND F IF IT IS FALSE:

25. The goal of preoperative cane is to prevent complications before, during and after surgery. T F

26. Surgery is done to remove a diseased body part or repair injured tissue. T F

27. Surgery often requires a hospital stay. T F

28. Women can wear jewelry to surgery. T F

29. Turning and repositioning are done every 3 to 4 hours after surgery. T F

30. An nurse anesthetist is an RN with advanced study giving anesthetics. T F

31. Artificial eyes and artificial limbs are removed before surgery. T F

32. Some surgeries require certain positions. T F

33. A surgical cap keeps hair out of the face and operative site. T F

34. Jewelries are worn to the operating room. T F

35. A full bladder can cause discomfort during a douche. T F

36. An open wound on the lower leg and feet caused by decreased blood flow through the arteries or veins is:

   A. Arterial Ulcer
   B. Decubitus ulcer
   C. Circulatory ulcer
   D. Pressure ulcer

37. Thin watery drainage that is blood-tinged is called:

   A. Sanguineous drainage
   B. Purulent drainage
   C. Serious drainage
   D. Serosanguineos drainage

38. Which is not a type of wound?

   A. Abrasion
   B. Gangrene
   C. Laceration
   D. Contusion

39. Partial-thickness wound caused by the scraping away or rubbing of skin is called:

   A. Incision
   B. Puncture wound
   C. Abrasion
   D. Penetrating wound

40. Violent act that injures the skin, mucous membranes, bones and internal organs is :

   A. Trauma
   B. Wound
   C. Shock
   D. Skin tear

41. Tissues are injured but she skin is not broken. This is called what?

A. Clean wound
B. Closed wound
C. Contaminated wound
D. Puncture wound

42. Dehiscence means:

A. Infected wound
B. Wounds with large amount of microbes
C. Wounds that does not heal easily
D. Separation of wound layers

43. A pressure ulcer can also be called:

A. Decubitus ulcer
B. Vascular ulcer
C. Venous ulcer
D. Hospital ulcer

44. An area where the bone projects from certain body surfaces is called...............?

A. Bedsore
B. Pressure sore
C. A bony prominence
D. Contusion

45. Which is not a bony prominence?

A. Shoulder blades
B. Sacrum
C. Ankles
D. Ear

46. Common causes of skin breakdown and pressure ulcers include the following except:

A. Friction
B. Shock
C. Shearing
D. Pressure

47. The bony areas are called:

    A. Bed sore
    B. Pressure sore
    C. Pressure areas
    D. Pressure stage

48. At the first stage of the pressure ulcers the skin is _____.

    A. Cyanosis
    B. Red
    C. Peels
    D. Cracks

49. Which is not a measure in preventing pressure ulcers?

    A. Positioning the person according to the care plan
    B. Raising the head of the bed to highest position
    C. Providing good skin care
    D. Minimizing skin exposure to moisture

50. Measures to prevent circulatory ulcers includes the following except:
    A. Keeping pressure off the heels and other bony areas
    B. massage over pressure points
    C. Keeping linens clean, dry and wrinkle free
    D. Dressing the person in tight clothes

51. Heat and cold application for promoting healing and comfort is ordered by:

    A. Doctor
    B. Nurse
    C. CNA
    D. Receptionist

52. Bluish skin color is also called_____-.

    A. Syncope
    B. Erythema
    C. Jaundice
    D. Cyanosis

53. A body temperature that is much higher than the person's normal is called..........

A. Hypothermia

B. Hyperthermia

C. Low blood pressure

D. Blood pressure rate

54. Heat applications are often used for:

A. Circulatory problems

B. Musculoskeletal injuries

C. Nervous Injuries

D. Heart Injuries

55. Which of the following is not a reason for heat application?

A. To relieve Pain

B. To increase joint stiffness

C. To reduce tissue swelling

D. To relax muscles

56. What type of application has greater and faster effects:

A. Dry heat application

B. Non-dry application

C. Heat application

D. Moist heat application

57. A cold application is usually between:

A. 50° to 65° F

B. 98° to 106° F

C. 100° to 106° F

D. 40° to 50° F

58. Heat and cold are applied for not longer than:

A. 2 to 5 minutes

B. 5 to 10 minutes

C. 15 to 20 minutes

D. 1 to 5 minutes

59. A very hot application is applied only by:

(A.) Charge Nurse
   B. Nursing assistant
   C. Physical therapist
   D. Occupational therapist

60. Very hot application is usually between:

   A. 95° to 108° F
   B. 106° to 120° F
   C. 105° to 106° F
   (D) 106° to 115° F

61. The Sitz bath usually last for:

   A. 5 minutes
   (B.) 20 minutes
   C. 45 minutes
   D. 50 minutes

62. An electric device used for dry heat is:

   A. Compress
   B. Compass
   (C) The aquachermia pad
   D. Hypothermia pad

63. Which one is not a sign and symptom of hypoxia?

   A. Dizziness
   B. Confusion
   (C.) Rash
   D. Fatigue

64. Hypoxia means _____.

   A. Rapid breathing
   (B) Insufficient oxygen to the cells
   C. Slow breathing
   D. Abnormal breathing

65. Smoking causes all the following except:

A. Lung cancer
B. Breath cancer
C. Kidney failure
D. Pressure ulcers

66. An early sign of hypoxia is:

A. Apprehension
B. Agitation
C. Cyanosis
D. Restlessness

67. Breathing deeply and comfortably only when sitting is called:

A. Dyspnea
B. Orthopnea
C. Apnea
D. Bradypnea

68. Slow, weak respirations fewer than 12 per minute is:

A. Cheyenne-strokes respirations
B. Biot's respiration
C. Respiratory depression
D. Respiratory arrest

69. Pulmonary function test measures:

A. The amount of oxygen in the blood
B. The amount of hemoglobin containing oxygen
C. The amount of air moving in and out of the lungs
D. How much air the heart can hold

70. A chest X-ray is taken to detect all the following except:

A. Foreign body in the thoracic cavity
B. Teeth damage
C. Fractures
D. Lung damage

71. A substance that gives off radiation is called:

A. Bronchoscopy

B. Thoracentesis

C. Radiation

(D) Radioisotope

72. Pulse oximetry measures:

(A) Oxygen concentration in arterial blood

B. The amount of brain damage

C. The capacity of air the lungs can hold

D. Measures progress of lungs disease.

73. Breathing is usually easier in one of these positions?

A. Sims's position

B. Prone position

(C) Fowler's Position

D. Supine position

74. Factors affecting oxygen needs include:

A. Respiratory system status

B. Aging

C. Pain

(D) All of the above

75. People with difficulty breathing often prefer sitting-up and leaning over a table to breathe. This is called:

A. Dorsal Recumbent position

B. Knee-chest position

(C) Orthopneic position

D. Lithotomy position

76. For individuals susceptible to decubitus ulcers, position changes are needed at least ....

A. q6h

(B) q2h

C. q3h

D. q8h

77. You are assisting a patient with coughing and deep breathing. Which is incorrect?

A. The person inhales through pursed lips
B. The person sits on comfortable position
C. The person holds a follow over air incision
D. The person inhales deeply through the nose

78. The collapse of a portion of the lungs is called:

    A. Pneumonia
    B. Dizziness
    C. Atelectasis
    D. Disorientation

79. A spirometer is a machine that measures:

    A. The movement of air
    B. The amount of air moving out of the lungs
    C. The volume of air exhaled
    D. The amount of air inhaled

80. The amount of oxygen to give and the device to use can only be ordered by _____.

    A. CNA
    B. Doctor
    C. RN
    D. LVN

81. Oropharyngeal airway is inserted through:

    A. Nostril and into the pharynx
    B. Nose and into the trachea
    C. The mouth and into the pharynx
    D. The surgically created opening into the trachea

82. Which one is not the upper part of the airway (Upper respiratory tract)?

    A. Mouth
    B. Pharynx
    C. Nose
    D. The trachea

83. Infection of the middle ear is called:

A. Otitis media
B. Deaf
C. Cerumen
D. Braille

84. Otitis media is common in _____.

   A. Adolescents
   B. Old people
   C. Infants
   D. Adults

85. A chronic disease of the inner ear is _____.

   A. Tinnitus
   B. Otitis media
   C. Acute Ear Disease
   D. Meniere's Disease

86. The middle ear contains Eustachian tube and three small bones called:

   A. Eardrum
   B. Tympanic membrane
   C. Ossicles
   D. Auditory canal

87. Difficulty in hearing normal conversation is _____.

   A. Tinitus
   B. Cerumen
   C. Vertigo
   D. Hearing loos

88. Hearing loss in which is impossible for the person to understand speech through hearing alone is _____.

   A. Deafness
   B. vertigo
   C. Tinnitus
   D. Otitis media

89. The most common cause of hearing loss in children is

A. Illness
B. Birth defects
C. Ear infection
D. Injury

90. Symptoms of hearing loss in children and adult include:

    A. Speaking too loudly
    B. Leaning forward to hear
    C. Asking for words to be repeated
    D. All of the above

91. Communicating with hearing impaired person includes the following except:

    A. Position yourself at the person's level
    B. Turn your back when speaking with the person
    C. Stand or sit in good sight.
    D. Speak clearly, distinctly and slowly

92. The second layer of the eyes is called:

    A. The sclera
    B. The retina
    C. The Choroid layer
    D. Optic nerve

93. The major cause of vision loss is _____.

    A. Otitis media
    B. Infections
    C. Glaucoma
    D. Hereditary

94. Hearing aids make:

    A. Sounds louder
    B. Speech clearer
    C. Correct hearing disorder
    D. Increase background noise

95. Braille involves:

A. Ringing in the ears
B. Raise dots arrange for letters of the alphabet
C. Dizziness
D. Audio Books

96. PCTs can provide safety for blind clients by doing the following except:

    A. Turning on lights
    B. Keeping doors open or closed
    C. Having client stand in the middle of room
    D. Informing the client of steps and curbs

97. When communicating with the speech impaired, you should do the following
    A. Listen, and give the person full attention
    B. Determine the subject been discussed
    C. Repeat what the person has said
    D. All of the above

98. _____ is a disease affecting the blood vessels that supply blood to the brain.

    A. Angina pectoris
    B. Myocardial infarction
    C. Stroke
    D. Heart attack

99. The third leading cause of death in the United States is _____.

    A. Heart attack
    B. Cerebrovascular accident
    C. Diabetes
    D. Obesity

100. The surgical creation of an artificial opening between the ureter and the abdomen is called:

    A. Ureterostomy
    B. Ileostomy
    C. Bosomy
    D. Colostomy

101. High sugar in the blood is called:

A. Hypoglycemia
B. Diabetes mellitus
C. Sugar Surge
D. Hyperglycemia

102. _____ is a tumor that grows fast and invades other tissues.

A. Fast tumor
B. Malignant tumor
C. Benign tumor
D. Metastasis

103. The removal of all or part of an extremity is _____.

A. Amputation
B. Decapitation
C. Evisceration
D. Cutting

104. Which therapy helps the immune system?

A. Hormone therapy
B. Chemotherapy
C. Biological therapy
D. Radiation therapy

105. The followings are the side effects of hormone therapy except:

A. Weight gain
B. Fatigue
C. Hot flashes
D. weight loss

106. Leukemia is the most common type of _____ in children.

A. Myocardial infarction
B. Cancer
C. Pneumonia
D. Stroke

107. Which of the followings can be a care for people with paralysis?

A. Keep the bed in low position
B. Follow bowel and bladder training programs
C. Maintain good alignment at all times.
D. All of the above.

108. _____ is spread by airborne droplets through coughing, sneezing, speaking, and singing.

A. Pneumonia
B. Leprosy
C. Asthma
D. Tuberculosis

109. The leading cause of death In United States is _____.

A. Coronary Artery Disease
B. Pneumonia
C. HIV
D. Angina

110. Which of the followings is the major complication of Coronary Artery Disease?

A. Emphysema
B. Dyspnea
C. Tuberculosis
D. Myocardial infarction

111. _____ occurs when the heart cannot pump blood normally.

A. Hypertension
B. Congestive heart failure
C. Hypotension
D. None of the above

112. Blood clot is also known as _____.

A. Bronchus
B. Thrombus
C. Blood stop
D. Platelets

113. The therapy that involves drugs that kill cancer cells is called:

A. Hormone therapy
B. Biological therapy
C. Chemotherapy
D. Physiotherapy

114. Using X-ray beams to destroy cancerous cells is _____ therapy.

A. Radiotherapy
B. Physiotherapy
C. Chemotherapy
D. Biological therapy

115. _____ is the spread of cancer to other parts of the body.

A. Stomatitis
B. Cancer transfer
C. Benign tumor
D. Metastasis

116. A condition in which there is the death of tissue is called:

A. Aphasia
B. Gangrene
C. Angina
D. Pectoris

117. _____ is when the bone becomes porous and brittle or is fragile and breaks easily.

A. Osteoporosis
B. Arthritis
C. Rheumatoid arthritis
D. Bone low density

118. Which of the followings is not a rule for cast care?

A. Turn the person every two hours
B. Wash the cast every 4hours
C. Elevate a casted arm or leg on pillows
D. Protect the person from rough cast edges.

119. Which of the followings is not a risk factor of stroke?

A. Smoking
B. Obesity
C. Exercise
D. Drug abuse

120. There are ___ major types of hepatitis.

A. 5
B. 3
C. 6
D. 4

121. Diseases that are contagious and infectious are called_____ diseases.

A. Non-communicable
B. Spreading
C. Communicable
D. Rapid

122. Which of the following is a sign or symptom of hepatitis?

A. Loss of appetite
B. Fever
C. Nausea and vomiting
D. All of the above

123. What type of diabetes occurs mostly in children?

A. Type 2
B. Type 3
C. Type 1
D. Type 4

124. Which of these is a sign of chronic renal failure?

A. Sudden severe headaches with no known cause
B. Halitosis
C. Rashes
D. Rigidity and trembling of extremities

125. The pathway created for urine to exit the body by removing the bladder is called _____.

A. Urinary Diversion
B. Urinary conversion
C. Urinary obstruction
D. Urinary bisection

126. Cystitis is a type of_____ infection.

A. Foot
B. Hair
C. Bladder
D. Mouth

127. Care of a person with stroke involves the following except:

A. The bed is kept in semi-Fowler's position
B. Avoid coughing and deep breathing.
C. Food and fluids needs are met
D. Good skin care prevents pressure ulcers

128. Psychosis means:

A. A state of severe mental impairment
B. Stomach
C. Lung Disorder
D. Heart disorder

129. Superego is concerned with_____.

A. Ability and disability
B. Mind and stress
C. Right and wrong
D. Health and illness

130. A vague uneasy feeling in response to stress is called:

A. Personality
B. Anxiety
C. Stress
D. Panic

131. Which one is not a sign and symptom of anxiety?

A. Rapid pulse
B. Rapid respiration
C. Increased blood pressure
D. Hyperthermia

132. Any factor that causes stress is called:

A. Obsession
B. Stress
C. A stressor
D. Phobia

133. The highest level of anxiety is _____.

A. Syncope
B. Panic
C. Dread
D. Terror

134. Which is not a sign and symptom of depression in older people?

A. Diarrhea
B. Paranoia
C. Dry mouth
D. Anxiety

135. Depression involves the following except:

A. Body
B. Mood
C. Euphoria
D. Thoughts

136. _____ occurs when a person is seeing, hearing or feeling something that is not real.

A. Delusion
B. Hallucination
C. Paranoia
D. Bipolar disorder

137. Mrs. White believes that she is the Queen of England. This is called a _____.

A. Hallucination
B. Paranoia
C. Delusion of persecution
D. Delusion of grandeur

138. Mr. Smith believes that his food is poisoned. This is called a _____.

    A. Superego
    B. Paranoia
    C. Psychosis
    D. Delusion

139. Anorexia nervosa occurs when?

    A. A person has an intense fear of weight gain and obesity
    B. Binge eating occurs
    C. A person explore his or her thoughts and feelings
    D. A person has severe extremes in mood

140. Repeating an act over and again without the ability to control the repetition is called:

    A. Ego
    B. Paraphrasing
    C. Compulsion
    D. Conscious

141. Delirium means:

    A. A false belief
    B. Loss of conjecture and social function
    C. Feeling something that is not real
    D. A state of temporary but acute mental confusion

142. Cognitive functioning includes all except:

    A. Memory
    B. Eating
    C. Thinking
    D. Reasoning

143. When caring for a confused person the PCT should do the following except:

A. Provide safety
B. Give date and time each morning
C. Rearrange Furniture and the person's view
D. Place familiar objects and pictures within the person's view

144. Loss of cognitive and social function caused by changes in the brain is called

A. Dementia
B. Paranoia
C. Obsession
D. Schizophrenia

145. Alzheimer's disease is:

A. Heart disease
B. Brain disease
C. Blood disease
D. Liver disease

146. The most common type of permanent dementia is _____.

A. Huntington's disease
B. Parkinson's disease
C. Alzheimer's disease
D. Korsakoff disease

147. The most common mental health problem in old people is

A. Depression
B. Infection
C. Drugs
D. Head injuries

148. Signs and symptoms of delirium include:

A. Tremors
B. Delusions
C. Hallucinations
D. All of the above

149. Mr. Fresh has delusion. Delusion means:

A. False dementia
B. False belief
C. A state of Temporary but acute mental confusion
D. Something that is not real

150. Signs, symptoms and behavior of Alzheimer's disease increase during:

   A. Daylight
   B. Morning time
   C. Early afternoon
   D. Hours of dark

151. The classic sign of Alzheimer's disease is _____-.

   A. Not recognizing objects
   B. Gradual loss of short term memory
   C. Agitation
   D. Mood and personality

152. The followings are common in people with Alzheimer's disease except

   A. Pain, rash and shock
   B. Communication problem, moodiness and restlessness
   C. Memory loss, poor judgment and poor reasoning
   D. Delusion, hallucination and screaming

153. When caring for Mr. Stone who is wandering you should do the following except:

   A. Follow agency policy for locking doors and windows
   B. Keep door alarms and electronic doors turned on
   C. Involve the person with activities
   D. Restraint Mr. Stone firmly

154. Mr. Jones becomes confused and begins to wander. The PCT should:

   A. Restrain him to prevent injuries
   B. Tell the doctor
   C. Report his behavior to the charge nurse
   D. Tell his family about the behavior

155. A common sign of depression is:
   A. Laughing and smiling
   B. Changes in appetite
   C. Socializing with friends

D. Attending activities

156. A mental disability occurring before 22years of age is called a _____.

A. Developmental disability
B. Mental retardation
C. Spastic
D. Spinal bifida

157. Mental retardation involves:

A. Violent sudden contractions of muscle groups
B. Muscle weakness
C. Low intellectual function
D. Uncontrolled contraction of skeletal muscles

158. These statements are true about cerebral palsy. Which one is false?

A. It is a disorder involving muscle weakness or poor muscle
B. It is violent contractions of muscle group
C. Lack of oxygen to the brain is the usual cause
D. The defect is in the motor region of the brain

159. Autism begins in early childhood between:

A. 12months and six years
B. 9 months and 7years
C. 10 months and 5years
D. 18 months and 3years

160. Paralysis of all four extremities is:

A. Paraplegia
B. Hemiplegia
C. Quadriplegia
D. Diplegia

161. Paralysis of one side of the body is

A. Quadriplegia
B. Hemiplegia
C. Paraplegia

D. Diplegia

162. Diplegia means:

(A) That similar body part are affected on both side of the body
B. The arm and leg on one side are affected
C. Both arms and both legs are paralyzed so are the trunks and neck muscles.
D. Paralysis of the leg or lower body

163. People with cerebral palsy have much impairment. They include the following except:

A. Mental retardation
B. Learning disabilities
C. Speech impairments
(D.) Wide flat nose

164. A chronic condition produced by temporary changes in the brains electrical function is:

A. Autism
(B.) Epilepsy
C. Spina bifida
D. Hydrocephalus

165. Seizures that occur in one part of the brain is called:

A. Whole seizures
B. Single seizures
(C.) Partial seizures
D. Generalized seizures

166. Spina bifida defects occur during the:

A. 3 months of pregnancy
(B.) First month of pregnancy
C. 6 months of pregnancy
D. 5 months of pregnancy

167. Down syndrome occurs:

A. First month of pregnancy
(B.) At fertilization
C. During birth
D. From trauma

168. Children with Down syndrome has certain features caused by extra chromosomes. They include the following except:

A. Drooling
B. Over shaped eyes that slant upwards
C. Flat face
D. Short, wide hands with stubby fingers

169. A seizure can also be called:

A. Autism
B. Down syndrome
C. Convulsion
D. Spina bifida

170. Spina bifida involves……………

A. Loss of consciousness
B. A defect of spinal column
C. Hearing impairments
D. Mental retardation

171. The inability of the male to have an erection is called:

A. Menopause
B. Impotence
C. Transvestite
D. Transsexual

172. Erectile dysfunction is same thing as:

A. Impotence
B. Menopause
C. Bisexual
D. Transsexual

173. Menopause is _____.

A. When the body responds to stimulation
B. When menstruation stops
C. Reproduce organ

D. Uniting of the sperm and ovum

174. Menstruation occurs about every:

A. 20 days
B. 18 days
C. 10 days
D. 28 days

175. Menopause occurs between _____ and _____ years of age.

A. 30 and 40
B. 30 and 35
C. 45 and 55
D. 50 and 60

CIRCLE T IF THE STATEMENT IS TRUE AND F IF IT IS FALSE.

176. Reproductive organs change with aging. T F

177. Diabetes and spinal cord injuries can cause impotence. T F

178. A heterosexual is a person who is attracted to both sexes. T F

179. Sexuality is important to small children. T F

180. Injury, Illness and surgery can affect sexual function. T F

181. Lochia means:

A. Person feelings and attitudes about his or her sex
B. Surgical removal of foreskin from the penis
C. Vaginal discharge that occurs after child birth.
D. Incision into perineum

182. Signs and symptoms of illness in babies include the followings except:

A. The body is limp and slow to respond
B. Lumps found in the breast
C. The body is flushed, pale or perspiring
D. The baby has reddened or irritated eyes

183. As a PCT you can help with breast feeding in the following ways:

A. Helping the mother to a comfortable position
B. Making sure the mother holds the baby close to her breast
C. Having the mother use her nipple to stroke the baby's cheek or lower lip.
D. All of the above

184. Breast-fed babies usually nurse every:

A. 8 or 12 hours
B. 4 or 8 hours
C. 2 or 3 hours
D. 3 or 6 hours

185. Babies are fed on:

A. Schedule
B. Demand
C. All time
D. On their mother's free time

186. Safety measures for infant includes the following except:

A. Laying an infant on fluffy bedding products.
B. Support the baby's head and neck when lifting or holding the baby
C. Handle the baby with gentle smooth movements
D. Use both hands to lift a newborn baby

187. A nursing mother needs:

A. Spicy and gas forming foods
B. Caffeine
C. Cola beverages
D. Good nutrition

188. Infant birth weight is the baseline for measuring:

A. Weight
B. Growth
C. Height
D. Amount of milk taken

189. When bathing a new born baby the water temperature should be _____ to _____ degrees F:

A. 80 to 90
B. 90 to 95
C. 100 to 105
D. 100 to 150

190. Which of the following is used to wash a new born baby's nose?

A. A mitted wash cloth
B. Cotton balls
C. Alcohol swipes
D. A cotton swab

191. A PCT should report the followings to the charge nurse when caring for new born babies except:

A. The baby has reddened or irritated eyes
B. The baby spit a small amount when burped
C. Stools are light-colored
D. The baby looks flushed, pale and perspiring

192. A baby's head and neck is always supported for the first_____ months.

A. 9
B. 6
C. 8
D. 3

193. When bottle-feeding babies. You should:

A. Prop the bottle and lay the baby down for the feeding
B. Force the baby to finish the bottle
C. Hold the baby close to you
D. Leave the baby at one inch with the bottle

194. Burping a baby is also called

A. Breast-feeding
B. Bubbling
C. Diapering
D. Circumcision

195. Newborns usually have a bowel movement with every feeding. T/F

196. Watery stools means constipation. T/F

197. Baby stops sucking and turns away from the bottle when satisfied. T F

198. You can lift a newborn by the arm. T/F

199. Moisture, feces, and urine irritate baby's skin. T F

200. Umbilical cord carries blood, oxygen and nutrients from the mother to fetus. T/F

201. A written plan listing the services needed by the person and who provides them is_____.

    A. Meal plan
    B. ADL plan
    C. A service plan
    D. Nursing Services

202. Assisted living provides the following except:

    A. Healthcare
    B. Skilled nursing care
    C. Housing
    D. Support services

203. The PCT should report any drug error to:

    A. RN
    B. Co-worker
    C. Receptionist
    D. Doctor

204. Medication records should include the following except:

    A. The person's name
    B. Number of wives
    C. Drug name, dose directions, and route of administration
    D. Date and time to take the drug

205. Which of the following is not drug error?

A. Taking the wrong dose
B. Taking another person's drug
C. Taking a drug when ordered
D. Taking a drug at the wrong time

206. Drugs are kept in:

A. Closet
B. On top of table
C. Under the bed
D. In a locked container, cabinet or area

207. Certain measures are needed when handling, preparing and storing food. It includes the following except:

A. Empty garbage at least once in two weeks
B. Protect left over foods
C. Wash cooking and eating items
D. Place washed eating and cooking items in a drainer to dry

208. A PCT can assist with drugs in the following ways except:

A. Reminding the person it is time to take the drug
B. Administering IV Therapy
C. Reading the drug label to the person
D. Opening containers for people who cannot do so

209. Transfer, discharge and eviction of person can happen for the following reasons:

A. The person fails to pay for services
B. The person wants to transfer
C. The facility closes
D. All of the above

210. Housekeeping measures help prevent infection in the following ways except:

A. Cleaning tub or shower after each use
B. Cleaning bathroom surfaces once in three weeks
C. Dusting furniture at least weekly
D. Vacuum floors at least weekly and as needed

211. When assisting with laundry services you should:

A. Follow your own preferences
B. Wash with hot water
C. Follow care label directions
D. Wash sturdy and delicate fabrics together

212. An assisted living resident is encouraged to eat in:

A. Dining room
B. Inner room
C. Bathroom
D. Kitchen

213. Which statement about assisted living is incorrect?

A. Assisted living provide secured and 24 hour supervision for residents
B. They provide each person with private apartment
C. Three meals a day and snacks are provided
D. They offer social and recreational service

214. Assisted facility residents have the right to:
A. Be treated with dignity respect, consideration and fairness
B. Help develop a plan
C. Receive the services stated in the service plan
D. All of the above

215. Which is not a requirement and features of assisted living facility units?

A. A mailbox for each person
B. A window that allow safe exit in an emergency
C. A closet with insects and rodents
D. Smoke detectors

216. The excessive loss of blood in a short time is called:

A. Blood flow
B. Blood loss
C. Hemorrhage
D. Blood clot

217. _____ occurs when the heart and breathing stop suddenly without warning.

A. System arrest
B. Heart malfunction
C. Cardiac Arrest
D. Heart stoppage

218. The emergency care given to an ill or injured person before medical help arrives is called:

A. Initial aid
B. First aid
C. Last Aid
D. Emergency aid

219. When breathing stops but heart action continues for several minutes. This is called:

A. Respiratory arrest
B. Heart arrest
C. Heart seizure
D. Heart failure

220. To activate EMS system, dial_____

A. 921
B. 112
C. 114
D. 911

221. Which is one of the goals of First Aid?

A. To cure the person permanently
B. To prevent injuries from becoming worse
C. To operate on the patient if the need arises there.
D. To make sure the person live at all cost

222. Causes of respiratory arrest include the following except:

A. Vomiting
B. Drowning
C. Smoke inhalation
D. Suffocation

223. Which of these is not a general rule of emergency care?

A. Check for life threatening problems

B. Stay calm
C. Do not hang up until the operator has hung up
D. Act with impulse

224. Which of the following is not a component of cardio-pulmonary resuscitation?

A. Airway
B. Breathing
C. Circulation
D. Medications

225. Which of these is not principle for chest compressions?

A. Massage the chest
B. Push fast
C. Massage the chest
D. Minimum of 100 compressions in one minute

226. _____ maneuver opens the airway.

A. Nose tilt
B. Stomach tilt
C. Head-tilt/chin
D. Nose-tilt/chin

227. The American Heart Association pediatric chain of survival involves these except:

A. Preventing cardiac arrest and injuries
B. Later advance care
C. Early CPR
D. Early access to emergency response system

228. When practicing CPR, we should use _____.

A. Babies
B. Adults
C. Young people
D. Mannequins

229. Cardiac arrest caused by heart disease is rare in _____.

A. Adults

B. Children
C. Young people
D. A and C

230. Which of these can lead to cardiac arrest?

A. Voiding
B. FBAO
C. Vomiting
D. None of the above

231. A large, poorly chewed piece of meat is a common cause of_____.

A. Syncope
B. Dying
C. Vomiting
D. Choking

232. Older people are at risk for choking. Which of these is not a risk?

A. Strong fitted dentures
B. Poorly fitted dentures
C. Dysphagia
D. Hard candy

233. _____ maneuver is used to relieve Chocking.

A. Parkinson
B. Einthoven
C. Heimlich
D. Chest

234. _____ results when organs and tissues do not receive enough blood.

A. Syncope
B. Shock
C. Convulsion
D. Cardiac Arrest

235. _____ is violent and sudden contractions or tremors of muscle group.

A. Shock
B. Syncope

C. Heart attack
D. Convulsion

236. Signs and symptoms of anaphylaxis are the followings except:

    A. Sweating
    B. Shortness of breath
    C. Voiding
    D. Dyspnea

237. Common causes of fires and burns include the following except:

    A. Cautions with matches and lighters
    B. Falling asleep while smoking
    C. Fireplaces
    D. Space heaters

238. _____ is the sudden loss of

    A. Stroke
    B. Fainting
    C. Cardiac failure
    D. Angina pectoris

239. _____ accident occurs when the brain is suddenly deprived of its blood supply.

    A. Cardio
    B. Reproductive
    C. System
    D. Cerebrovascular

240. The Heimlich maneuver is performed with people in one the following positions:

    A. Standing
    B. Sitting
    C. Walking
    D. Lying

241. A document stating a person's wish about healthcare when the person cannot make his or her own decisions is _____.

A. Emergency directives

B. Later directives

C. Advance directives

D. Healthcare directives

242. Post mortem means:

A. During death

B. After Death

C. Before death

D. Death

243. The belief that the spirit or soul is reborn in another body or in another form of life is

_____.

A. Resurrection

B. Ascension

C. Awakening

D. Reincarnation

244. There _____ stages of Grief.

A. 5

B. 3

C. 4

D. 7

245. When diagnosed with brain cancer, Mr. Blue responds "NO NOT ME", what griefing stage is he in?

A. Anger

B. Depression

C. Denial

D. Bargaining

246. _____ care focuses on the physical, emotional, social, and spiritual needs of dying people and their families.

A. Hospital

B. Hospice

C. Covalent

D. Clinic

247. _____ wills is a document about measures that support or maintain life when death is likely.

A. Person
B. Living
C. Dying
D. Facility

248. The dying person's room should have the following conditions except:

A. The PCT arrange the room as they wish
B. The room should be comforting and pleasant
C. The room should be well lit and well ventilated
D. The room should reflect the person's choice

249. MRS. Smith is a dying patient and suddenly says "This is not true, I know that I am dreaming.....". Which dying stage is this_____?

A. Acceptance
B. Depression
C. Denial
D. Bargaining

250. The dying person bill of right includes the following except:

A. I have the right to be treated as a living human being till I die
B. I have the right not to be deceived
C. I have the right to die with somebody
D. I have the right to die in peace and dignity

251. Restraints are used only if ordered by a _____.

A. Charge nurse
B. Doctor
C. Therapist
D. CNA

252. When the dying person engages you in conversation. As the PCT you should do the following except:

A. Let the person express feelings and emotions.
B. Do not worry about saying the wrong thing or finding comforting words.

C. Ignore the client
D. Listen carefully and don't interrupt

253. Dying People often need the following except:

   A. Hospital care
   B. Nursing center
   C. Hospice
   D. Sports center

254. The Stiffness or rigidity of skeletal muscles that occurs after death is called:
   A. Post mortem stiffness
   B. Rigor Mortis
   C. Mortem
   D. Mortis

255. _____ illness or injury is one for which there is no reasonable expectation of recovery.
   A. Sudden
   B. Emergency
   C. Terminal
   D. Mortem

Section Three Questions (EKG)

   1. The heart is a hollow muscular organ located in the thoracic cavity between the lungs in a space called?
      a. Sternum
      b. Mediastenum
      c. Heart Chamber
      d. Lungs

   2. The heart Base is located at the level of the _____ intercostal?
      a. 1st
      b. 2nd
      c. 4th
      d. 5th

   3. The heart Apex is located at the level of the _____ intercostal?
      a. 1st
      b. 2nd
      c. 4th

d. 5th

4. The function of the _____ is to prevent blood cell destruction and clotting?
   a. Endocardium
   b. Myocardium
   c. Pericardium
   d. Epicardium

5. _____ is made up of four rings of connecting tissue?
   a. Heart Skeleton
   b. Myocardium
   c. Pericardium
   d. Epicardium

6. _____ is not a characteristic of the atrioventricular valves?
   a. Tough fibrous rings
   b. Long and strong leaflets
   c. Half-moon shaped leaflets
   d. They have accessory organs

7. The mitral valve is also known as?
   a. Middle valve
   b. Atria valve
   c. Atrioventricular valve
   d. Bicuspid

8. _____ is not a characteristic of the semilunar valves?
   a. Three leaflets
   b. Shallow in depth
   c. They have no accessory organs
   d. Tough fibrous rings

9. The _____ are the first branches coming out of Aorta and supply the heart with oxygenated blood
   a. Pulmonic valve
   b. Right and left coronary arteries
   c. Right Ventricles
   d. Left Ventricles

10. _____ is the period of contractions of both Arial and Ventricles?
    a. Diastole
    b. Systole
    c. Cardiac cycle
    d. Heart physiology

11. _____ is the period of relaxation and filling of all cardiac chambers?
    a. Diastole
    b. Systole
    c. Cardiac cycle
    d. Heart physiology

12. _____ are caused by diseases of the valves or other structural abnormalities?
    a. Left Anterior Descending
    b. Murmurs
    c. Left Circumflex
    d. Diastole

13. The normal heart rate is?
    a. 40-60 bpm
    b. 60-100 bpm
    c. 80-100 bpm
    d. 100-120 bpm

14. The Heart Rate is controlled by Chemo-receptors and _____ located in Aortic Arch and Carotid arteries?
    a. Baro-receptors
    b. Bio-receptors
    c. Physio-receptors
    d. Chemo-arteries

15. Parasympathetic generally has an inhibitory effect via the neurotransmitter Acetylcholine which may cause the following to happen except?
    a. Slows SA pacemaker and HR
    b. Slows the conduction of electricity in AV node
    c. Increases the force of contraction
    d. Decreases the strength of atrial and ventricular contraction

16. Sympathetic via the neurotransmitter Norepinephrine results in the following except?
    a. Increases the Heart Rate
    b. Decreases the strength of atrial and ventricular contraction
    c. Increases the blood pressure
    d. Via dopaminergic receptors increases the diameter of the visceral blood vessels and consequently the visceral blood flow

17. The blood volume ejected outside the heart is equal to the blood volume _____?
    a. Lost from the heart
    b. Present in the heart
    c. Returning back into the heart
    d. All of the above

18. _____ is the blood volume ejected outside the ventricle after each contraction?
    a. Heart Pump
    b. Sympathetic
    c. Parasympathetic
    d. Stroke Volume

19. _____ is the amount of blood ejected outside the heart per minute?
    a. Cardiac Output
    b. Stroke Volume

c. Blood pressure
d. None of the above

20. _____ is the force exerted by circulating blood volume on the walls of the artery during circulation?
    a. Cardiac Output
    b. Stroke Volume
    c. Blood pressure
    d. Heart Pump

21. The formular for calculating Cadiac output is?
    a. (Stroke volume) x (HR per/min) / 100
    b. (Stroke volume) / (HR per/min)
    c. (Stroke volume) x (HR per/min)
    d. (HR per/min) / (Stroke volume)

22. The formular for calculating Cadiac output is?
    a. (Cardiac Output) x (Vascular Resistance) /100
    b. (Vascular Resistance) / (Cardiac Output)
    c. (Cardiac Output) / (Vascular Resistance)
    d. (Cardiac Output) x (Vascular Resistance)

23. Which of the following is not true?
    a. Higher Cardiac output will result in a higher BP
    b. Lower vascular resistance will result in a higher BP
    c. Lower cardiac output will result in a lower BP
    d. High vascular resistance will also result in a higher BP

24. _____ is the force exerted against the blood flow and is determined by the diameter of the vessel?
    a. Cardiac Output
    b. Peripheral Vascular Resistance
    c. Blood pressure
    d. Stroke Volume

25. _____ occurs when positively charged ions rapidly move from outside the myocardial cell membrane to the inside, changing the overall charge from negative to positive?
    a. Contractility
    b. Depolarization
    c. Repolarization
    d. Conductivity

26. _____ occurs immediately after depolarization and is the movement of positively charged ions back to the outside of the cell, returning the cell back to its original polarized state?
    a. Contractility
    b. Absolute Refractory Period
    c. Repolarization
    d. Conductivity

27. The 1st phase of repolarization in which a myocardial cell is unable to react to any electrical stimulus is called?
     a. Contractility
     b. Absolute Refractory Period
     c. Relative Refractory Period
     d. Conductivity
28. The 2nd phase of repolarization during which time a strong enough electrical stimulus might cause new depolarization and contraction is called?
     a. Contractility
     b. Absolute Refractory Period
     c. Relative Refractory Period
     d. Conductivity

29. The Conduction system of the heart consists of the following except?
     a. Bundle of His
     b. Purkinje fibers
     c. SV node
     d. Bundle branches

30. In the AV node, there is normally a _____ second delay of electrical activity to allow blood to flow from the atria and fill the ventricles with blood?
     a. .10 - .20
     b. .12 - .20
     c. .15 - .30
     d. .02 - .10

31. _____ is the system that generates and delivers electricity to all the muscle fibers of the heart?
     a. Automaticity
     b. Excitability
     c. Conductivity
     d. Conduction system of the heart

32. Which of this is not an important EKG tool for patient's diagnosis and evaluation?
     a. Evaluates injuries to the heart muscle
     b. Evaluate the response toward medication
     c. Monitoring patient's HR
     d. Evaluates the Heart Electricity

33. _____ is a wire that connects the electrode to the EKG machine?
     a. Cable
     b. Heart wire
     c. Lead
     d. Electrode wire

34. _____ is a recorded tracing of the heart electricity from one or two electrodes that provides a specific view of the heart?
     a. Cable
     b. Heart wire

c. Lead

d. Electrode wire

35. _____ is a paper, plastic or metal sensor placed on the patient's skin on a specific location and transmits it to the cable?

    a. Cable

    b. Heart wire

    c. Lead

    d. Electrode

36. All of the following lead types records electrical activity in the frontal plane except?

    a. Standard Bipolar Limb Leads

    b. Augmented Unipolar

    c. Precordial Chest Unipolar Leads

    d. Basic Leads

37. _____ lead records the heart electricity from one limb and compare it with a zero voltage lead in the center of the heart?

    a. Standard Bipolar Limb Leads

    b. Augmented Unipolar

    c. Precordial Chest Unipolar Leads

    d. Basic Leads

38. What does AV stand for?

    a. Augmented Voltage

    b. Atrium Volume

    c. Augmented Volume

    d. Arm Voltage

39. The positive electrodes on the 5th intercostal space, left midclavicular line is?

    a. V1

    b. V3

    c. V4

    d. V6

40. The positive electrodes on the 4th intercostal space, right sternal border is?

    a. V1

    b. V3

    c. V4

    d. V6

41. The positive electrodes on the 5th intercostal space, midaxillary line is?

    a. V1

    b. V2

    c. V5

    d. V6

42. Which of the following records electrical activity in the horizontal plane?

    a. Standard Bipolar Limb Leads

    b. Augmented Unipolar

c. Precordial Chest Unipolar Leads
d. Basic Leads

43. Which of the following is not a characteristics of "P wave"?
    a. It is produced by atrial repolarization
    b. It is smooth and round
    c. Not more than 2.5 mm high and no more than 0.11 sec
    d. Positive in I,II, and V2 to V6

44. Which of the following is not a characteristic of "QRS complex"?
    a. It represents ventricular repolarization
    b. The ventricle is depolarized from the endocardium to the myocardium, to the epicardium.
    c. Normal duration is no more than 0.1 sec
    d. None of the Above

45. Which of the following is not a characteristic of "T wave"?
    a. It is a deflection produced by ventricular repolarization.
    b. It is slightly asymmetric
    c. It is smooth
    d. It is not more than 5 mm in height

46. Which of the following is not a characteristic of "U wave"?
    a. Represents repolarization of Purkinje fibers
    b. Round and symmetric
    c. A prominent U wave is due to hypokalemia
    d. It is more 1.5 mm in height

47. The segment that is measured from the end of the P wave to the beginning of the QRS complex is called?
    a. ST
    b. TU
    c. PQ
    d. PR

48. The segment that represents the time of ventricular contraction and the beginning of repolarization of both ventricles is?
    a. ST
    b. TU
    c. PQ
    d. PR

49. _____ segment is the most sensitive part of EKG changed by cardiac ischemia.
    a. ST
    b. TU
    c. PQ
    d. PR

50. _____ is measured from the beginning of QRS to the end of T wave?
    a. ST Segment
    b. PR Interval

    c. J Junction

    d. QT Interval

51. _____ Is defined as P wave and PR segment?
    a. ST Segment
    b. PR Interval
    c. J Junction
    d. QT Interval

52. _____ represents the total ventricular activity (ventricular depolarization PLUS ventricular repolarization)?
    a. ST Segment
    b. PR Interval
    c. J Junction
    d. QT Interval

53. What segment is compared to the PR segment to help identify myocardial ischemia or injury
    a. ST Segment
    b. PR Interval
    c. J Junction
    d. QT Interval

54. Which of this is not a step to follow when analyzing the EKG strip for its quality and to identify any emergency pathology?
    a. Examine the P waves
    b. Assess Rhythm
    c. Examine the J Junction
    d. Assesses the Heart Rate

55. Which of the following is not a method used when assessing heart rate?
    a. Counting Method
    b. 300 sec. Method
    c. 6 sec. Method
    d. Large Box Method

56. When assessing the heart rate, what method is used when you count the number of large boxes between two consecutive RR and divide into 300 for the ventricular rate?
    a. Counting Method
    b. 300 sec. Method
    c. 6 sec. Method
    d. Large Box Method

57. Which of this is not a characteristic of the normal sinus rhythm?
    a. Diastolic pause is longer
    b. Heart rate 60 – 100 bpm
    c. Similar P in all the leads in front of all QRS
    d. A constant PR (0.12 to 0.2) sec interval in all the leads, regular rhythm

58. Which of this is not a characteristic of the Sinus Tachycardia?

a. Heart rate over 100 bpm
b. Similar P in all the leads in front of all QRS
c. Diastolic pause is very small or nonexistent
d. Tachycardia reduces the blood supply to the cardiac muscle

59. Which of this is not a characteristic of the Sinus Bradycardia?
    a. Heart rate 60 – 100 bpm
    b. Normal equal P and QRS in all the leads, as well as normal PR intervals
    c. Diastolic pause is longer
    d. Bradycardia decreases the blood flow in the brain and other body tissues

60. _____ is caused by an irritable focus in the atria that fires electrical impulses after the normal firing of the SA node pacemaker.
    a. AV Reentry Tachycardia
    b. Sinus Tachycardia
    c. Atrial Tachycardia
    d. Sinus Arrhythmia

61. _____ is caused when the electrical impulse passes through a passage other than AV node
    a. AV Reentry Tachycardia
    b. Sinus Tachycardia
    c. Atrial Tachycardia
    d. Sinus Arrhythmia

62. Which of this is not a characteristic of the Atrial Flatter?
    a. No identifiable P waves can be seen
    b. Rapid depolarization of a single atrial focus at a rate of 250-350 bpm.
    c. Slower ventricular rate
    d. Typical saw-toothed waves

63. Which of this is not a characteristic of the Atrial Fibrillation?
    a. Controlled atrial fibrillation, average ventricular rate is less than 100 bpm.
    b. Uncontrolled atrial fibrillation, average ventricular rate is over 100 bpm.
    c. It is caused by multiple irritable sites all over the atria firing at a rate exceeding 350 bpm
    d. Typical saw-toothed waves

64. Which of this is not a characteristic of the Ventricular Tachycardia?
    a. Regular fast rhythm 100 to 250 bpm
    b. No P waves
    c. Wide, bizarre QRS complexes with T waves pointing in opposite direction from main QRS direction
    d. Atrial rate is greater than ventricular rate

65. The total absence of ventricular electrical activity is called?
    a. AV Block
    b. Asystole
    c. Ventricular Tachycardia
    d. Ventricular Fibrillation

66. _____ is defined as a delay or interruption of the electric impulse conduction beyond the AV node?
    a. AV Block
    b. Asystole
    c. Ventricular Tachycardia
    d. Ventricular Fibrillation

67. The type of AV block that is also called a Complete Heart Block is the?
    a. Fourth degree AV block
    b. Second degree AV block
    c. Fifth degree AV block
    d. Third degree AV block

68. _____ is defined as an insufficient blood supply to the myocardium?
    a. Infarction
    b. Ischemia
    c. Myocardia
    d. Subendocardia

69. _____ is the common cause of blood supply reduction to the myocardium?
    a. Atherosclerosis of the coronary arteries
    b. Myocardial infarction
    c. Ischemia
    d. Subendocardia

70. _____ is defined as sudden death of the myocardial tissue due to an abrupt cessation of the blood flow?
    a. Atherosclerosis of the coronary arteries
    b. Myocardial infarction
    c. Ischemia
    d. Subendocardia

71. The World Health Organization **(WHO)** criteria for the diagnosis of myocardial infarction are the presence of at least two of the following, which of this is not a criteria?
    a. Clinical history of ischemic-type of chest discomfort
    b. Changes on serial EKG tracings
    c. Rise and fall in serum cardiac markers demonstrating cardiac tissue damage.
    d. None of the above

72. Wandering baseline can be caused by which of the following condition?
    a. Patient's tremors
    b. Sweat or lotion on the patient's skin
    c. Electrical appliances or apparatus being used nearby while the tracing is taken.
    d. Loose electrode or cables or by frayed or broken wires

73. _____ can produce jittery patterns on the EKG tracing?
    a. Somatic tremors
    b. Artifact
    c. 60-cycle interference

d. Broken recording

74. _____ is an unwanted interference or jitter on the EKG recording?
    a. Somatic tremors
    b. Artifact
    c. 60-cycle interference
    d. Broken recording

75. _____ is caused by improperly grounded electrical equipment that is directly or indirectly in contact with the patient?
    a. Somatic tremors
    b. Artifact
    c. 60-cycle interference
    d. Broken recording

76. _____ can be caused by a damaged wire or loose electrodes?
    a. Somatic tremors
    b. Artifact
    c. 60-cycle interference
    d. Broken recording

77. Which of the following is a sympathetic drug used to manage cardiac arrest, because increases heart contractibility?
    a. Isuprel
    b. Lidocaine
    c. Epinephrine
    d. Intropin

78. _____ is used in the treatment of paroxysmal supraventricular tachycardia (PSVT), effective in terminating more than 90% of episodes of PVST in adults and infants?
    a. Nitroglycerin
    b. Morphine Sulfate
    c. Digitalis
    d. Verapamil

79. Patients who takes _____requires constant monitoring for signs and symptoms of toxicity such as yellow vision, nausea, vomiting, and drowsiness?
    a. Nitroglycerin
    b. Morphine Sulfate
    c. Digitalis
    d. Verapamil

80. _____ is the drug of choice for the suppression of ventricular ectopy, including ventricular tachycardia and ventricular flutter?
    a. Nitroglycerin
    b. Metoprolol
    c. Lidocaine
    d. Verapamil

81. _____ is useful in preventing atrial fibrillation, atrial flutter, and paroxysmal supra-ventricular tachycardia?
    a. Nitroglycerin
    b. Metoprolol
    c. Lidocaine
    d. Verapamil

82. _____ produces an overall increase in heart rate and myocardial contractility?
    a. Epinephrine
    b. Dopamine
    c. Isoproterenol
    d. Dopamine

83. _____ is a traditional drug of choice for the pain and anxiety associated with acute myocardial infarction?
    a. Morphine Sulfate
    b. Nitroglycerin
    c. Metoprolol
    d. Lidocaine

84. _____ when in high doses, may cause respiratory depression?
    a. Morphine Sulfate
    b. Nitroglycerin
    c. Metoprolol
    d. Lidocaine

85. _____ is a powerful smooth muscle relaxant effective in relieving angina pectoris
    a. Nitroglycerin
    b. Metoprolol
    c. Dopamine
    d. Isoproterenol

86. The _____ plane divides the body horizontally into an upper and lower part?
    a. Sagittal
    b. transverse plane
    c. frontal plane
    d. Midsagittal

87. In the Positional and Directional Terms "Prone" means?
    a. Lying of the Back
    b. Lying on the Belly
    c. Back side of the Body
    d. Away from the surface

88. In the Medical Terminology the prefix **"dia-"** means?
    a. Two
    b. Die
    c. Complete
    d. Deficient

89. In the Medical Terminology the prefix **"Hypo-"** means?
   a. Over
   b. Under
   c. More than Normal
   d. Less than Normal

90. In the Medical Terminology the suffix **"-dynia"** means?
   a. Blood Condition
   b. Die
   c. Two
   d. Pain

91. In the Medical Terminology the suffix **"-osis"** means?
   a. Inflammation
   b. Protein
   c. Condition
   d. Disease

92. The possibility of exposure to toxic, carcinogenic or caustic substances is a _____ safety hazard
   a. Biologic
   b. Sharp
   c. Chemical
   d. Physical

93. Biological Hazards can be caused by
   a. Bacterial infections
   b. needles, lancets, and broken glass
   c. wet floors and heavy lifting can
   d. high-voltage equipment

94. In the Healthcare Terminology what are some combining forms for HEAD?
   a. Cephal/o
   b. Cerebr/o
   c. Hepat/o
   d. Cyt/o

95. In the Healthcare Terminology what are some combining forms for KIDNEY?
   a. Oste/o
   b. Rhin/o
   c. Thromb/o
   d. Ren/o

96. In the Healthcare Terminology what are the meaning of this combining forms **Nephr/o**
   a. Head
   b. Kidney
   c. Disease
   d. Flesh

97. In the Healthcare Terminology what are the meaning of this combining forms **Iatr/o**
   a. Liver

b. Treatment

c. Iron

d. Intestine

98. In the Healthcare Terminology what are the meaning of this combining forms **Sarc/o**

    a. Stomach

    b. Nose

    c. Flesh

    d. Skin

99. Personal Protective Equipment includes all EXCEPT?

    a. Masks

    b. Goggles

    c. Trash Bags

    d. Boots

100. Bacteria, fungus or parasites can be classified under what type of hazard:

    a. Emotional

    b. Physical

    c. Chemical

    d. Biological

Section Four (Phlebotomy)

In this section, we would be using the term 'phlebotomist' because the phlebotomist is an individual trained to draw blood. It is within the scope of patient care technicians to draw blood if they receive the required training.

1. The following are roles of the phlebotomist except:

    a. Collect routine capillary and venous specimens for testing as requested.

    b. Prepare specimen for transport, ensuring its stability.

    c. Give medication prescriptions on any blood related disorder.

    d. Transport specimen to the laboratory

2. Standards of right and wrong called the _____ provide personal and professional rules of performance and moral behavior that all phlebotomists are expected to follow.

    a. Honesty

    b. Integrity

    c. Code of Ethics

        d. Professional appearance

3. _____is a system which carries deoxygenated blood from the right ventricle to the lungs and returns oxygenated blood from the lungs to the left atrium
        a. Pulmonary circulation
        b. The heart
        c. Systemic circulation
        d. Circulatory system

4. Which type of circulation carries oxygenated blood from the left ventricle throughout the body.
        a. Pulmonary circulation
        b. The heart
        c. Circulatory system
        d. Systemic circulation

5. Each side of the heart (right and left) is composed of an upper chamber called
        a. the ventricle
        b. atrium
        c. Vein
        d. The pulmonic valve

6. _____ is a semi lunar valve situated between the right ventricle and the pulmonary artery
        a. The pulmonic valve
        b. the ventricle
        c. atrium
        d. The tricuspid valve

7. _____ is an atrioventricular valve, being situated between the right atrium and right ventricle
        a. The pulmonic valve
        b. mitral valve
        c. The aortic valve
        d. The tricuspid valve

8. _____ is an atrioventricular valve, being situated between the left atrium and left ventricle
        a. The pulmonic valve
        b. mitral valve
        c. The aortic valve
        d. The tricuspid valve

9. The heart has _____ layers
        a. One
        b. Two
        c. Three
        d. Four

10. A semi lunar valve situated between the left ventricle and the aorta.
        a. The pulmonic valve
        b. mitral valve
        c. The aortic valve

     d. The tricuspid valve

11. The coronary arteries, which supply blood to the heart, are found in which layer.
     a. fibrous outer layer of the heart
     b. The muscular middle layer
     c. The endothelial inner layer lining of the heart
     d. Myocardium

12. The endothelial inner layer lining of the heart is called
     a. Myocardium
     b. Endocardium
     c. Epicardium
     d. The Capillaries

13. The muscular middle layer of the heart is
     a. Myocardium
     b. Endocardium
     c. Epicardium
     d. Mitral valve layer

14. _____ is the fibrous outer layer of the heart
     a. Myocardium
     b. Endocardium
     c. Epicardium
     d. Mitral valve layer

15. The blood vessels, except for _____ , are composed of three layers
     a. Aorta
     b. arteries,
     c. arterioles
     d. capillaries

16. Which of these combinations carry oxygenated blood from the heart to the various parts of the body?
       i. aorta, arteries,
      ii. venules,
      iii. veins
      iv. Arterioles

     a. i and iii
     b. iv , I and iii
     c. I and iv
     d. Ii and iii

17. All BUT ONE carry deoxygenated blood back to the heart.
     a. venules,
     b. aorta
     c. veins
     d. superior and inferior vena cava

18. The _____, composed only of a layer of endothelial cells, connect the arterioles and venules.
    a. Capillaries
    b. Aorta
    c. Arteries
    d. Tissue cells

19. The average adult has
    a. 5 to 6 liters of blood
    b. 10 to 15 litres
    c. 5 to 6 Gallons of blood
    d. 10 to 12 gallons of blood

20. The liquid portion of the blood is called?
    a. Formed element
    b. Plasma
    c. Electrolyte
    d. Cellular portion

21. The plasma contains all the following BUT
    a. Proteins
    b. Hydrochloric acids
    c. Gases
    d. Hormones

22. Red blood cells is known as
    a. Thrombocytes
    b. Leukocytes
    c. Electrolyte
    d. Erythrocytes

23. White blood cells is known as
    a. Thrombocytes
    b. Leukocytes
    c. Electrolyte
    d. Erythrocytes

24. The platelets is known as
    a. Thrombocytes
    b. Leukocytes
    c. Electrolyte
    d. Erythrocytes

25. The normal life span of Red Blood Cell is?
    a. 120 days
    b. 90 days
    c. 360 days
    d. 30 days

26. The reticulocyte takes one to two days to mature into?
    a. Thrombocytes
    b. Leukocytes
    c. erythrocyte
    d. Platelets

27. _____ is a situation with increased White Blood Cells?
    a. Leukopenia
    b. Erythropenia
    c. Erythrocyte dehydration
    d. Leukocytosis

28. _____ is a situation with decreased White Blood Cells?
    a. Leukopenia
    b. Erythropenia
    c. Erythrocyte dehydration
    d. Leukocytosis

29. These are types of White Blood Cells in the blood except?
    a. Neutrophils
    b. Lymphocytes
    c. Karyocytes
    d. Basophils

30. _____ carry histamine, which is released in allergic reactions?
    a. Neutrophils
    b. Lymphocytes
    c. Karyocytes
    d. Basophils

31. _____ represent 1% to 3% of the WBC population. They are active against antibody-labeled foreign molecules. Their numbers are increased in allergies, skin infections, and parasitic infections.
    a. Neutrophils
    b. Lymphocytes
    c. Eosinophils
    d. Basophils

32. The second most numerous, comprising about 20% to 40% of the WBC population. Their number increases in viral infection, and they play a role in immunity is known as?
    a. Neutrophils
    b. Lymphocytes
    c. Eosinophils
    d. Basophils

33. _____ is the process by which blood vessels are repaired after injury?
    a. Hemostasis
    b. Chemotherapy
    c. Leukocytosis
    d. Neutrophils

34. Hemostasis occurs in four stages; in what order
    i. Vascular phase
    ii. Coagulation phase
    iii. Fibrinolysis
    iv. Platelet phase
    a. I, ii, iii, iv
    b. I, iii, iv, ii
    c. ii, iii, i, iv
    d. I,iv,ii,iii

35. During venipuncture _____ is the most suitable or the vein of first consideration?
    a. Cephalic vein
    b. Median cubital vein
    c. Basilic vein
    d. Thrombotic veins

36. _____ is an impermeable pad used to protect the patient's clothing and bedding?
    a. Chux
    b. Gloves
    c. Tourniquets
    d. Vacutainer needles

37. The most common complication of phlebotomy procedure is?
    a. Phlebitis
    b. Hematoma
    c. Hemoconcentration
    d. Trauma

38. The increase in proportion of formed elements to plasma caused by the tourniquet being left on too long. (More than two (2) minutes)
    a. Phlebitis
    b. Hematoma
    c. Hemoconcentration
    d. Trauma

39. Thrombus is a complication when:
    a. insufficient pressure is applied after the withdrawal of the needle causing blood clot
    b. There are tiny non-raised red spots that appear on the skin from rupturing of the capillaries due to the tourniquet being left on too long or too tight.
    c. Inflammation of a vein with formation of a clot
    d. systemic infection associated with the presence of pathogenic organism is introduced during a venipuncture

40. Inflammation of a vein as a result of repeated venipuncture on that vein is known as _____
    a. Phlebitis
    b. Petechiae
    c. Septicemia
    d. Trauma

41. _____is the permanent surgical connection between an artery and a vein
    a. Fistula
    b. Edema
    c. Fasting
    d. Septicemia

42. _____ is the accumulation of fluid in the tissues
    a. Fistula
    b. Edema
    c. Fasting
    d. Septicemia

43. Below are Factors To Consider Prior To Performing The Procedure except for_____
    a. Fistula
    b. Edema
    c. Fasting
    d. Hematoma

44. Quality control actually starts _____is collected from the patient
    a. While the specimen
    b. before the specimen
    c. after the specimen
    d. anytime the specimen

45. Which of the following ANALYTICAL ERRORS relates to AFTER COLLECTION of blood
    a. Improper use of serum separator
    b. Wrong order of draw
    c. Hemolysis
    d. Inadequate fast

46. Which of the following ANALYTICAL ERRORS relates to BEFORE COLLECTION of blood
    a. Improper use of serum separator
    b. Wrong order of draw
    c. Hemolysis
    d. Inadequate fast

47. Which of the following ANALYTICAL ERRORS relates to DURING COLLECTION of blood?
    a. Exposure to light
    b. Patient posture
    c. Under filling tubes
    d. Medication interference

48. Which of the following statement is FALSE as regards ROUTINE VENIPUNCTURE
    a. Verify the requisition for the tests
    b. Identify the patient: check the patient's ID number and have him/her state his/her name
    c. Identify yourself to the patient, explain the procedure, and assume you got his/her consent
    d. Palpate the veins in the antecubital fossa using your index finger

49. Which of the following statement is TRUE as regards ROUTINE VENIPUNCTURE

a. Palpate the vein while looking for the straightest point. Cleanse the area using a straight motion starting at the inside of the venipuncture site.
b. Palpate the vein while looking for the straightest point. Cleanse the area using a Circular motion starting at the inside of the venipuncture site.
c. With the bevel facing downward, insert the needle at an angle of 15-30 degrees.
d. Hold the patient's arm, by placing four fingers over the forearm and your thumb above the antecubital area slightly pulling the skin back to anchor the vein

50. The tourniquet should not be left on for more than _____ minute(s) in order to prevent hemoconcentration, from the time blood flow begins
    a. one
    b. three
    c. five
    d. ten

51. Discard needle into the:
    a. biohazards sharp container
    b. Polythene bag
    c. Leather bag
    d. Trash bin

52. At any point when the bleeding stops, an adhesive bandage is applied over folded gauze square. The patient should be instructed to:
    a. Keep the bandage for a day or two
    b. remove the bandage within an hour
    c. apply more pressure to the venipuncture area to speed up recovery
    d. change the adhesive bandage to a non-adhesive bandage after about five hours

53. Below are the routine that should be performed after the venipuncture is completed EXCEPT:
    a. Remove gloves
    b. wash your hands
    c. say good-bye to the patient
    d. deliver the results

54. Which of the following statement is correct
    a. You can label the tubes prior to the venipuncture
    b. You can leave the patient's room before labeling the tubes
    c. You can dismiss an outpatient After labeling the tubes
    d. You can label tubes using a pencil; black ink should be used

55. _____ test is used to diagnose diabetes mellitus and evaluate patients with frequent low blood sugar
    a. Therapeutic Drug Monitoring
    b. Oral Glucose Tolerance Test
    c. Timed Specimens
    d. Fasting Specimens

56. _____ used to monitor the level of a specific substance or condition in the patient
    a. Therapeutic Drug Monitoring
    b. Oral Glucose Tolerance Test
    c. Timed Specimens

        d. Fasting Specimens

57. _____ requires collection of blood while the patient is in the basal state
        a. Therapeutic Drug Monitoring
        b. Oral Glucose Tolerance Test
        c. Timed Specimens
        d. Fasting Specimens

58. It is the responsibility of the _____ to verify if the patient indeed, has been fasting for the required time.
        a. Medical Assistant
        b. Phlebotomist
        c. Doctor
        d. Nurse

59. The test is used to monitor the blood levels of certain medication to ensure patient safety and also maintain a plasma level is called
        a. Therapeutic Drug Monitoring
        b. PKU
        c. Timed Specimens
        d. Fasting Specimens
60. They are ordered to detect presence of microorganisms in the patient's blood.
        a. Blood Cultured test
        b. Two-Hour Postprandial Test
        c. PKU
        d. Timed Specimens

61. All but one requires chilled specimen under special specimen handling:
        a. arterial blood gases,
        b. lactic acid,
        c. Two-Hour Postprandial Test
        d. parathyroid hormone.

62. The following precautions should be observed when performing dermal puncture
        a. Do not puncture deeper than 2.0mm
        b. Do not perform dermal punctures on previous puncture sites
        c. do not use the back of the heel or arch of the foot
        d. All of the Above

63. Often requests are for more than one test to be performed; and as such, more than one collection tube needs to be drawn. The correct order of draw is

        i.   blood culture tubes or vials
        ii.   EDTA tubes (e.g., lavender tops)
        iii. sodium citrate tubes (e.g., blue tops)
        iv.   Oxalate/ fluoride tubes (e.g., gray tops).
        v.   serum tubes with or without clot activator or gel
        vi.   heparin tubes

a. i, ii, iii, iv, v, vi
b. I, iii, v, vi, ii, iv
c. I, iii, iv, v, vi, ii
d. I, iii, vi, v, iv, ii

64. _____ analyzes plasma levels of drugs and poisons.
    a. Electrophoresis
    b. Toxicology
    c. Immunochemistry
    d. None of the above

65. _____ analyzes chemical components of blood such as hemoglobin and serum, urine and cerebrospinal fluid, based on the differences in electrical charge
    a. Electrophoresis
    b. Toxicology
    c. Immunochemistry
    d. All of the above

66. The section where blood is collected, stored and prepared for transfusion is known as
    a. Blood Bank Section
    b. Serology (Immunology) Section
    c. Microbiology Section
    d. Urinalysis Section

67. Physical examination in the Urinalysis section does not evaluates
    a. color,
    b. pH
    c. clarity
    d. Specific gravity

68. Serology (Immunology) Section
    a. is responsible for the detection of pathogenic microorganisms in patient samples and for the hospital infection control
    b. performs tests on the urine to detect disorders and infection of the kidney and urinary tract and to detect metabolic disorders such as diabetes mellitus
    c. Performs tests to evaluate the patient's immune response through the production of antibodies
    d. This is the section where blood is collected, stored and prepared for transfusion.

69. The possibility of exposure to toxic, carcinogenic or caustic substances is a _____ safety hazard
    a. Biologic
    b. Sharp
    c. Chemical
    d. Physical

70. Biological Hazards can be caused by
    a. Bacterial infections

b. needles, lancets, and broken glass
c. wet floors and heavy lifting can
d. high-voltage equipment

71. _____ occurs when there is insufficient return of blood flow to the heart, resulting in inadequate supply of oxygen to all organs and tissues of the body
    a. Shock
    b. External Hemorrhage
    c. Biological hazard
    d. Chemical hazard

72. Common symptoms of shock includes:
    a. Pale, cold, clammy skin
    b. Rapid, weak pulse
    c. Increased, shallow breathing rate
    d. All of the above

73. _____ are infectious microorganisms that can be classified into groups namely: viruses, bacteria, fungi, and parasites.
    a. Portal of exit
    b. Patients
    c. Agents
    d. Portal of entry

74. Which of these is a mode of transmission?
    a. Contact : direct and indirect
    b. Droplet
    c. Airborne
    d. All of the above

75. What is the most important means of preventing the spread of infection?
    a. Medical Asepsis
    b. Barrier Protection
    c. Hand washing
    d. Isolation Precautions

76. The Acronym CPR stands for?
    a. Cardiovascular Prompt Resuscitation
    b. Cardiopulmonary Resuscitation
    c. Careful Patient Revival
    d. Cardiopulmonary Rescue

77. The use of various chemicals that can be used to destroy many pathogenic microorganisms can be referred to as?
    a. Isolation Precautions
    b. Barrier Protection
    c. Disinfection
    d. Contact precautions

78. The sharps injury log must NOT NECESARILY contain, at a minimum:

a. The type and brand of device involved in the incident.
b. The department or work area where the exposure incident occurred.
c. The Account Number/Financial Information of the injured person.
d. An explanation of how the incident occurred

79. Informed consent is
    a. Consent given by the patient who is made aware of any procedure to be performed, its risks, expected outcomes, and alternatives.
    b. consent given by the Medical Professional to the patient about the procedure to be performed
    c. Consent given by the patient who is unaware of any procedure to be performed, its risks, expected outcomes, and alternatives.
    d. Consent given by the patient after the procedure is performed.

80. The failure to exercise the standard of care that a reasonable person would give under similar circumstances and someone suffers injury because of another's failure to live up to a required duty of care can be called
    a. Patient confidentiality breach
    b. Professional Negligence
    c. Lack of Experience
    d. Tort

81. *Defamation of character, Invasion of privacy, and Battery can be classified under*
    a. Patient confidentiality breach
    b. Professional Negligence
    c. Lack of Experience
    d. Tort

82. All but one is not a component of the chain of infection,
    a. Susceptible host
    b. Portal of Settlement
    c. Source
    d. Mode of transmission
    e.

83. Personal Protective Equipment includes all EXCEPT
    a. Masks
    b. Goggles
    c. Trash Bags
    d. Face Shields Respirator

84. Bacteria, fungus or parasites can be classified under what type of hazard:
    a. Emotional
    b. Physical
    c. Chemical
    d. Biologic

85. Which is the correct order of hemostasis?
    i. Vascular phase
    ii. Coagulation phase
    iii. Platelet phase
    iv. Fibronolysis
    a. iv, ii, iii,i

b. i, ii, iii,iv

c. i,iii,iv,ii

d. I,iii,ii,iv

86. Which of these veins is suitable for venipuncture
    a. Tortuous
    b. Thrombotic veins
    c. Cephalic vein
    d. Sclerosed veins

87. The _____of the bore of the Vacutainer needle is referred to as the gauge
    a. Radius
    b. Length
    c. Diameter
    d. Breadth

88. _____ is an injury to underlying tissues caused by probing of the needle
    a. Trauma
    b. Petechiae
    c. Septicemia
    d. Hematoma

89. Rimming clots is a(n)
    a. Before Collection analytical error
    b. During Collection analytical error
    c. After Collection analytical error
    d. None of the above

90. Poor coordination with other treatments is a(n)
    a. Before Collection analytical error
    b. During Collection analytical error
    c. After Collection analytical error
    d. None of the above

91. Which of the following statement is FALSE when performing dermal puncture for Infant
    a. Do not puncture deeper than 2.0mm
    b. Do not perform dermal punctures on previous puncture sites
    c. Do not use the medial and lateral areas of the plantar surface of the heel
    d. Do not use the back of the heel or arch of the foot.

92. What is the proper Order of draw for capillary specimens?
    1. Lavender tube 2. Tubes with other additives 3. Tubes without additives
        a. 1,2,3
        b. 2,1,3
        c. 3,2,1
        d. 1,3,2

93. Electrophoresis
    a. Uses techniques such as radio immunoassay (RIA) and enzyme immunoassay to detect and measure substances such as hormones, enzymes, and drugs.

b. analyzes chemical components of blood such as hemoglobin and serum, urine and cerebrospinal fluid, based on the differences in electrical charge analyzes plasma levels of drugs and poisons

c. analyzes plasma levels of drugs and poisons

d. enumerating and classifying the red blood cells, white blood cells, and platelets

94. Which of the following statements about Shock is incorrect?
    a. Patients experiencing trauma may go into shock
    b. Expressionless face/staring eyes is a common symptom of shock
    c. Keep the victim warm until help arrives is good first aid measure
    d. Keep the victim lying down with the head higher than the rest of the body

95. The blood vessels, except for the _____, are composed of three layers
    a. Capillaries
    b. Arteries
    c. Venules
    d. superior and inferior vena cavae

96. Post-prandial means:
    a. Fasting
    b. Before a meal
    c. After a meal
    d. Before bedtime

97. Which of the following Statement is FALSE?
    a. Needle disposal container must be a clearly marked puncture-resistant biohazard disposal container.
    b. Never recap a needle without a safety device.
    c. It is best to draw blood from an arm with IV fluids running into it
    d. Always wash hands properly after every blood draw procedure

98. The "Good Samaritan Law" encourages healthcare professionals to
    a. Wait for authorization to help victims in emergency
    b. Provide medical care within the scope of their training at the scene of an accident without fear of being sued for negligence.
    c. To provide blood and money to the minors and senior citizens
    d. Be composed and alert at all times

99. _____ are tiny non-raised red spots that appear on the skin from rupturing of the capillaries due to the tourniquet being left on too long or too tight.
    a. Petechiae
    b. Hematoma
    c. Hemoconcentration
    d. Septicemia

100. Failure to obtain blood may be caused by a tube loosing it vacuum. This may be due to all the following EXCEPT
    a. A manufacturing defect
    b. Expired tube
    c. The transparency of the tube
    d. A very fine crack in the tube

SECTION FIVE

1. Which of these is not a guideline for completing a job application?
   A. Read and follow the directions.
   B. Lying on an application.
   C. Write neatly.
   D. Give information about employment gap.

2. Courtesy is?
   A. Behavior in the work place.
   B. Seeing things from other person's point of view.
   C. Polite or helpful comment or act.
   D. Feeling sorry for a person.

3. Work ethics involves the following except:
   A. How others walk.
   B. How you look.
   C. What you say.
   D. How you behave.

4. Good work ethics involves these qualities and traits except:
   A. Gossiping.
   B. Dependable.
   C. Courteous.
   D. Trustworthy.

5. The response or change in the body caused by any emotional, physical, social or Economic factor is:
   A. Sleep.
   B. Weight.
   C. Drugs.
   D. Stress.

6. Stress can be reduced by one of the following:
   A. Planning personal and quite time.
   B. Shouting and screaming.
   C. Judging yourself harshly.
   D. Blaming yourself for thing you did not do.

7. The best response to an interview question is:
   A. Long answers.
   B. Short answers.

C. "Yes" or "No".
D. Brief explanation.

8. All are common interview questions except:
   A. Tell me about yourself.
   B. Tell me about your career goals.
   C. Where do you study?
   D. How do you set priorities?

9. Which of these is not a good behavior during a job interview?
   A. Sitting in a professional manner.
   B. Touching or reading things on the interviewer's desk.
   C. Good eye contact with an interviewer.
   D. Maintaining good body language.

10. One of these is NOT professional speech and language:
    A. Speaking softly and gently.
    B. Speaking clearly.
    C. Cursing and yelling.
    D. Good relationship with the person and family.

11. Good hygiene for work involves the followings:
    A. Bathing daily.
    B. Using a deodorant or antiperspirant.
    C. Keeping fingernails clean, short and neatly shaped.
    D. All of the above.

12. Practices for a professional appearance involves the following except:
    A. Practice good hygiene.
    B. Wear uniform that fit well.
    C. Wear jewelry in pierced eyebrows and nose.
    D. Wear your name badge or photo ID at all times when on duty.

13. How should a PCT dress for a job interview?
    A .Wearing a clean t-shirt and casual slacks.
    B. Wearing a business attire or well ironed scrubs
    C. Wearing formal attire.
    D. Wearing a tank top.

14. All employers want employees who are:
    A. Dependable.
    B. Well-groomed.
    C. Have the needed job skills and training.
    D. All of the above.

15. Guidelines for job safety practices include the followings except:
    A. Understanding the roles, functions and responsibilities in your job Description.
    B. Know the contents and policies in personnel and procedure manuals.
    C. Gossiping with co-workers.

D. Know what you can and cannot do.

16. These statements are true about gossip. Which one is false?
    A. Gossip spreads rumors.
    B. Gossip is hurtful.
    C. Gossip is to talk about the private matters of others.
    D. Gossip is professional and not hurtful.

17. A co-worker tells you that a nurse and patient are dating. This is?
    A. Confidential information.
    B. Gossip.
    C. Sexual harassment.
    D. Eavesdropping.

18. Keeping personal matters out of the work place includes the followings except
    A. Making personal phone calls only during meals and breaks.
    B. Controlling your emotions.
    C. Discussing personal problems at work.
    D. Turn off personal pagers or wireless phone while at work.

19. When planning your work you should do the following except:
    A. Discuss priorities with the nurse.
    B. Know the routine of your shift and nursing unit.
    C. Leave a messy work area.
    D. Judge how much time you need for each person, procedure and task.

20. To trouble, torment, offend or worry a person by one's behavior or comment
    is called?
    A. Stress.
    B. Harassment.
    C. Courtesy.
    D. Gossip.

21. These statements signal a bad attitude except:
    A. "Please show me how this works."
    B. " I work harder than anyone else."
    C. "No one appreciates what I do."
    D. I can't. I'm too busy."

22. Which one is not a common reason for losing a job?
    A. Using offensive speech and language.
    B. Stealing the agency's or person's property.
    C. Having weapons in the work setting.
    D. Having good values and attitudes that fit the agency.

23. The best definition of a patient care assistant is a:

A. Person who transcribes the doctor's order for patient care.
    B. Licensed person who provides education about special diets.
    C. Person who is certified to give care under the direct supervision of a licensed personnel

D. Graduate nurse who is registered and licensed by the the state to practice nursing.

24. A nurse who has completed a 2-,3-, or 4-year nursing program and has passed a board exam is a:

A. Licensed vocational nurse.
B. Registered nurse.
C. Physician.
D. CNA

25. Which of the following is not a member of long-term healthcare team?

A. Charge nurse.
B. Nursing supervisor.
C. Receptionist.
D. Nursing assistant.

26. As a patient care assistant, your important role in meeting standards and survey process includes:

A. Providing quality care.
B. Protecting the person's rights.
C. Conducting yourself in a professional manner.
D. All of the above.

27. The purpose of a long-term care facility is:

A. To provide emergency care for blind people.
B. To provide care for persons who cannot care for themselves at home.
C. To provide surgical care for mental people
D. None of the above.

28.   A sudden illness from which a person is expected to recover is?
A. Chronic illness.
B. Terminal illness.
C. Acute illness.
D. Hospice.

29. The goal of rehabilitation and restorative care is to:
A .Return persons to their highest possible level of physical and psychological functioning.
B. Worsen resident's condition.
C. Do surgery.
D. Provide clients with privacy.

30. All long-term care nurse aids must be evaluated for competency and must complete

a distinct educational course, these requirement are set by:

A. OBRA
B. HIPAA
C. OSHA
D. CDC.

31. Who assists person to learn or retain skills and designs adaptive equipment needed to perform activities of daily living?

A. Nursing assistant.
B. Medical technologist(MT).
C. Dietitian.
D. Occupational therapist(OT).

32. Responsibilities of a PCT are listed in a:

A. Job title.
B. Job description.
C. Job credentials.
D. Procedure.

33.   The purpose of health care is to:

A. Promote good health.
B. Prevent disease.
C. Detect and treat disease.
D. All of the above

34. A healthcare payment program sponsored by federal & state government is:

A. Medicaid.
B. Healthcare.
C. Insurance.
D. Team care.

35. Any item, object, device, garment, material or drug that limits or restricts person's freedom of movement or access to one's body is _____.

A. Protector.
B. Safety guide
C. A restraint
D. Device

36. Restraints are for the following people except:

A. Confused person
B. Blind people
C. Person with behavior problem

D. People who has poor judgment

37. Which is not a risk of restraints use?
    A. Shock
    B. Depression
    C. Bruises
    D. Fractures

38. Discipline is any action that:

    A. Controls the person's behavior
    B. Requires less effort by the agency
    C. Is not in the person's best interest
    D. That punishes or penalizes a person

39. According to OBRA and CMS, physical restraints includes these except:

    A. Is attached to or next to the person's body
    B. Controls mental function
    C. Restricts freedom of movement or access to one's body
    D. Cannot be easily removed by the person

40. Physical restraints are applied to the following places except:

    A. Chest
    B. Waist
    C. Eyes
    D. Wrists

41. These are risks of restraint use except:

    A. Agitation
    B. Dehydration
    C. Cuts
    D. Trust

42. Information about restraints is recorded in the person's _____.

    A. Nursing history
    B. Medical record
    C. Intake and output chart
    D. Graph sheet

43. Leather restraints are applied to_____.

    A. Wrists and ankles
    B. Eyes and head
    C. Mouth and nose
    D. Mouth and fingers

44. When charting you should include the following information:

    A. The type of restraint applied
    B. The body part or parts restrained
    C. The reason for the application
    D. All of the above

45. Wrists restraints limit_____ movements.

    A. Hip
    B. Leg
    C. Arm
    D. Finger

46. The straps of vest and jacket restraints always cross in:

    A. Centre
    B. Side
    C. Front
    D. Back

47. The safety belt is always in_____ angle.

    A. 45
    B. 100
    C. 25
    D. 10

48. Vest and jacket restraints are applied to the:

    A. Wrists
    B. Chest
    C. Hand
    D. Leg

49. Ms. Walsh has a restraint on her waist. You should check the position of the restraint at least:

    A. Every 3hours
    B. Every 30 minutes
    C. Every 2hours
    D. Every 15 minutes

CIRCLE T IF THE STATEMENT IS TRUE AND F IF IT IS FALSE

50. Wrist restraints are used to prevent fall. T F

51. Restraints are used when the nurse thinks it is needed. T F

52. Restraints are made of cloth or leather. T F

53. Some drugs are restraints. T F

54. Passive physical restraint does not totally restrict freedom of movement. T F

55. Restraints can increase confusion and agitation. T F

56. Restraints must be snug and firm, but not tight. T F

57. A vest restrains crosses at the back. T F

58. Tight restraints affect circulation and breathing. T F

59. Entrapment can occur between the bars of a bed rail. T F

60. Restraints require a doctor's order. T F

61. Every agency has policies and procedures for restraint use. T F

62. You can apply restraints when you think they are needed. T F

63. Older people are restrained more than younger people. T F

64. Restraints are used only once as a last resort to protect people from harming themselves or others. T F

65. The administration of a vaccine to produce immunity against an infectious disease is called?
    A. Vaccination
    B. Vaccine
    C. Immunity
    D. Clean technique

66. The process of destroying all microbes is_____.

    A. Germicide
    B. Disinfection
    C. Sterile
    D. Sterilization
67. Hand washing is one way to prevent the spread of infectious agents' through_____.

    A. Droplet
    B. Airborne transmission
    C. Direct contact
    D. Food and water

68. Which of the following is not a sign or symptom of infection

    A. Fever
    B. High blood pressure

C. Nausea

D. Rash

69. Medical asepsis is the same as:

A. Normal flora

B. Surgical asepsis

C. Sterile technique

D. Clean technique

70. Protection against a certain disease is called:

A. Personal protective equipment

B. A germicide

C. Immunity

D. A vaccine

71. Between routine resident contacts, the PCT should wash his/her hands under running water for at least_____

A. 10-15 seconds

B. 30 minutes

C. 5-6 minutes

D. 60 seconds

72. Standard precautions apply to;

A. Persons with infections

B. All doctors

C. All people

D. All residents

73. Microorganism grows best in_____.

A. Moist places

B. Hot environment

C. Dry places

D. High temperature

74. A wet or moist mask is _____.

A. Safe

B. likely contaminated

C. Clean

D. Sterile

75. Masks are used for_____ precautions.

A. Standard

B. Isolation
C. Airborne
D. Contact

76. HIV and HBV are found in:

A. Blood
B. Intestine
C. Heart
D. Feces

77. HIV and hepatitis B are examples of a _____.

A. Rickettsia
B. Virus
C. Protozoa
D. Fungi

78. Hepatitis B is a _____ disease.

A. Kidney
B. Heart
C. Liver
D. Lungs

79. Asepsis means:

A. Being free of disease-producing microbes
B. Medical asepsis
C. Process of destroying pathogens
D. Protection against certain disease.

Circle T if the statement is true and F if it is false:

80. Gloves can be reused. T F

81. Masks prevent spread of microbes from the respiratory tract. T F

82. Specimens are transported to the laboratory in biohazard specimen bags. T F

83. All linen bags need a biohazard symbol. T F

84. Nosocomial infections are acquired during a stay in a health facility. T F

85. Unused Items in a person's room are used for another person. T F

86. A sterile package is contaminated when the expiration date has passed. T F

87. Isolation precaution prevents the spread of contagious diseases. T F

88. A pathogen can cause an infection. T F

89. Microbes need a reservoir to live and grow. T F

90. Using the body in an efficient and careful way is called:
    A. Base of support
    B. Posture
    C. Body mechanics
    D. Log rolling

91. These factors lead to back disorders except:

    A. Turning whole body when changing direction of your movement.
    B. Reaching while lifting.
    C. Poor posture when sitting or standing.
    D. Twisting while lifting.

92. Ergonomics is the science of_____.

    A. Balance
    B. Body Alignment
    C. Designing the job to fit the worker
    D. Using body in an efficient way.

93. Which is a function of the muscles to the body?

    A. Movement of body parts.
    B. Bearing of the body weight.
    C. Protects the organs.
    D. Pumps blood to the heart.

94. To change direction, a patient care aid should:

    A. Move her body in section.
    B. Mover her body slowly.
    C. Twist from the waist.
    D. Turn her whole body by moving her feet.

95. When repositioning a heavy client, the PCT should:

    A. Move the client alone
    B. Get a Co-Worker
    C. Move the client hater
    D. Get the family move the client.

96. Turning the person as a unit, in alignment with one motion is called:

    A. Body Alignment

B. Ergonomics
C. Folding
D. Logrolling.

97. Stretchers are used to transport people who are_____.

A. Disabled
B. Cannot sit up
C. Are mentally ill
D. Unsteady

98. A transfer belt is applied_____.

A. Over clothing
B. Over bare skin
C. Over the breast
D. For the chest

99. As a PCT you should reposition a patient or resident at least every:

A. 3hours
B. 15 minute
C. Every 2 hours
D. 30 minutes

100. Lying on the abdomen with the head turned to one side is _____ position?

A. Lateral
B. Sims
C. Supine
D. Prone

101. In a semi-sitting position the head of the bed should be raised between_____ and _____.

A. 50degrees, 100degrees
B. 45degrees, 150 degrees
C. 100 degrees, 150 degrees
D. 45degrees, 90 degrees

102. In what position should unconscious patients be positioned when giving oral care?

A. Lateral position
B. Sims' position
C. Supine position
D. Prone position

103. To transfer a patient with a mechanical lift, at least_____

A. One staff member is needed
B. Twelve staff members are needed

C. Two staff members are needed

D. Five staff members are needed

104. These statements are about positioning. Which one is incorrect?

    A. Good position makes breathing easier and circulation is promoted.

    B. It causes skin break down.

    C. Proper positioning's helps prevent pressure ulcers and contractures

    D. Regular position changes and good alignment promote comfort and well-being.

105. Which is not a guideline to safely position a person?

    A. Use good body mechanics

    B. As a co-worker to help you if needed

    C. Twisting while moving the person

    D. Explain the procedure to the person.

106. Transferring a client from a bed to a stretcher requires that the PCT use:

    A. Proper body mechanics

    B. Gait belt

    C. Minimum of 5 workers

    D. A Hoyer lift.

107. As a PCT when transferring a client from the bed to the wheelchair you should always_____

    A. Place the paper or sheet under the person's feet

    B. Lock the brakes on the wheelchair first.

    C. Unlock the brakes on the wheel chair

    D. Use mechanical lift.

108. Dangling a client's leg over the side of is done to:

    A. To prevent pressure sores.

    B. Give the client time to put on shoes

    C. Make sure is able to sit up first.

    D. Prevent orthostatic hypotension

109. Using a broad base of support means?

    A. Keeping the feet comfortably apart

    B. Keeping objects close to your body

    C. Bending and reaching

    D. keeping knees locked in place

110. When having a client to sit-up and dangle his legs before walking, the PCT should observe the following except:

    A. Increased Respiration

B. Cheerfulness

C. Excessive sweating

D. Sudden paleness

111. Another name for transfer belt is _____ .

A. Mechanical belt

B. Hoyer Lift

C. Gait belt

D. Waist belt

112. The rubbing of one surface against another is called:

A. Friction

B. Sharing

C. Logrolling

D. Posture

113. The left side lying position in which the upper leg is sharply flexed so it is not on the lower leg is called?

A. Supine position

B. Lateral Position

C. Prone position

D. Sims' position

114. Which of these can be used to lift and move the person in bed and reduce friction?

A. A spread

B. Drawsheet

C. A sheet

D. Blanket

115. The head of the bed is lowered, and the foot of the bed is raised, this position is called?

A. Fowler's position.

B. Semi-fowler's position.

C. Reverse tredelenburg's   position.

D. Tredelenburg's position.

116. To prevent odor you should do the followings except:

A. Keeping laundry container open.

B. Changing soiled linen and clothing's promptly.

C. Checking incontinent person often.

D. Disposing of incontinence and ostomy products promptly.

117. People who are ill are sensitive to drafts, As a PCT to protect them you should do the followings except:

A. Make sure they wear the correct clothing.

B. Always leave them on drafty areas.

C. Cover them with blankets.
D. Offer lap blankets to those in chairs and wheelchairs.

118. OBRA requires that nursing centers should maintain a temperature range of:

    A. 40 to 50 degrees Fahrenheit.
    B. 100 to 150 degrees Fahrenheit.
    C. 30 to 50 degrees Fahrenheit
    D. 71 to 81 degrees Fahrenheit

119. Which people are more sensitive to cold?

    A. Older people
    B. Younger people
    C. Disabled people
    D. Blind people

120. The patient and resident may find sounds dangerous, frightening or irritating, to decrease noise you should_____

    A. Control your voice
    B. Answer phones, signal lights and intercoms promptly
    C. Handle equipment properly
    D. All of the above

121. Good lightning is need for:

    A. Low temperature
    B. Blood circulation
    C. Safety and comfort
    D. Ventilation

122. Dull lightning can cause the following except:

    A. Falls
    B. Brain problem
    C. Headaches
    D. Eyestrain

123. People with poor vision needs_____.

    A. Dim light
    B. Dull light
    C. Bright light
    D. No Light

124. Raising bed horizontally to give care reduces_____.

A. Bending and reaching
B. Twisting and jerking
C. Lifting and moving
D. Sitting and standing

125. Flatbed position is used after _____.

A. Spinal cord injury
B. Surgery
C. Cervical traction
D. all of the above

126. When the head of the bed is raised to 3o degrees and the knee portion is raised 15 degrees; what position is this?

A. Fowler's
B. Semi-fowler
C. Trendelenburg's
D. Prone

127. Having the means to be completely free from the public view while in bed is_____>

A. In visual privacy
B. Curtain down privacy
C. Full visual privacy
D. Isolation

CIRCLE T IF IS TRUE AND F IF IT IS FALSE

128. OBRA requires that nursing center rooms be as homelike as possible. T F

129. People restricted to certain positions may need their bed locked. T F

130. Locking feature is useful for people with confusion or dementia. T F

131. Residents cannot bring some furniture and personal items from home. T F

132. Privacy curtains prevent others from seeing the person. T F
133. The overbed table and bedside stand should be within the person's reach. T F

134. Signal light should always be within the person's reach, in the room, bathroom and tub room. T F

135. A small sheet placed over the middle of bottom sheet is called:

A. Draw sheet
B. Fitted sheet
C. Top sheet
D. Mattress

136. A piece of linen that is placed beneath the client from shoulders to thigh is _____ .

    A. An underpad
    B. Blanket
    C. A drawsheet
    D. A sheet

137. When making a bed, the PCT should place the soiled linen:

    A. On the Resident's closet
    B. In a laundry bag
    C. On the floor
    D. on the bedside table

138. The PCT should always hold linens_____ .

    A. Close to their chest
    B. On their heads
    C. Towards their body
    D. Away from their body and uniform.

139. Clean linens are placed on_____ .

    A. Clean surface
    B. On the floor
    C. Dirty surface
    D. Laundry containers

140. A surgical bed should be left in what position?

    A. Lowest position
    B. Semi-fowler's position
    C. Highest Position
    D. Fowler's position

141. When changing wet, damp, or soiled linens, you should always wear …………

    A. Face shields
    B. Gloves
    C. Masks
    D. Protective apparel

142. Which is not a rule for bed making?

    A. Shaking linens before use
    B. Use good body mechanics
    C. Follow the rules of medical asepsis
    D. Follow standard precautions and the blood borne pathogen standard.

143. The type of bed made for a person who is taken by the stretcher to treatment or therapy is called:

   A. The closed bed
   B. Open bed
   C. Surgical bed
   D. Occupied bed

144. Bed made for people who are out of their beds is called:

   A. Occupied bed
   B. Open bed
   C. Close bed
   D. Surgical bed

SECTION SIX

1. AM care is care that is given:

   A. After lunch
   B. Before lunch
   C. Before breakfast
   D. After breakfast

2. H.S is care that is given at what time?

   A. Before bed time
   B. After meal
   C. Before meal
   D. Upon awakening

3. As a PCT, the first step in performing any procedure is to _____.

   A. Provide privacy
   B. Explain the procedure
   C. Perform hand washing
   D. Introduce yourself by name and title

4. Before dressing a client the PCT should first:

   A. Report to charge nurse
   B. Provide privacy
   C. Choose the client's clothes
   D. Check the order

5. Gloves must be worn when:

   A. Feeding the a patient
   B. When combing a resident's hair
   C. Making bed
   D. Providing Peri-care

6. Afternoon care involves the following except:

   A. Assisting with elimination
   B. Cleaning incontinent people
   C. Brushing client's teeth
   D. Changing wet or soiled linens and garments.

7. The medical abbreviation for 'before the meal' is_____.

   A. qid
   B. a.c
   C. p.c
   D. bid

8. It is important to always practice standard precaution when_____.

   A. Dressing a patient
   B. Providing oral hygiene
   C. Ambulating a patient
   D. Feeding a patient

9. The safe water temperature for complete bed bath is_____.

   A. 50° F
   B. 80° F
   C. 110° F
   D. 150° F

10. The purpose of perineal care is to

    A. Prevent skin breakdown
    B. Prevent infection
    C. Prevent itching, burning and body odor
    D. All of the above

CIRCLE T IF THE STATEMENT IS TRUE AND F IF IT IS FALSE

11. Odors and discomfort occur if perineal areas are not clean. **T** F

12. Back massages last 3 to 5 minutes. T F

13. Lotion reduces friction during massage. T F

14. Fowler's position is best for a massage. T F

15. Back massage relaxes muscles and stimulates circulation. T F

16. The normal water temperature for perineal care is 150ºF. T F

17. Perineal care is also done whenever the area is soiled with urine and feces. T F

18. Perineal area is delicate and easily injured. T F

19. Weak people can be left alone in the shower if they are sitting down. T F

20. Flossing removes plaque and tartar from the teeth. T F

21. Perineal care helps prevent infection and body odor. T F

22. Excessive body hair in women and children is called:

    A. Hirsutism
    B. Alopecia
    C. Pediculosis
    D. Dandruff

23. Brushing and combing hair are part of_____ care.
    A. Afternoon care
    B. Night care
    C. Morning care
    D. Midnight care

24. When giving hair care to a client you should place the towel:

    A. On the client's leg
    B. At her/his back
    C. On the stomach
    D. Across the shoulder

25. The PCT should record and report the following observation:

    A. Normal appearance
    B. Length of hair
    C. Flaking
    D. Presence of lice

26. Nail and foot care prevents the following except:

    A. Infection
    B. Injury

C. Fall

D. Odors

27. The first rule when changing client's gown and clothing is:

A. Provide privacy
B. Encourage the person to do as much as possible
C. Let the person choose what to wear
D. Raising the bed for body mechanics

28. When changing clothing, you need the following information from the nurse and care plan except:

A. How much help the person needs.
B. If the person needs to wear certain garments.
C. What observations to report and record.
D. How many clothes the patient has.

29. What observation do you need to report and record when giving nail and foot care?

A. The shape of the nails.
B. Any abnormalities.
C. Any complaints by the person
D. All of the above.

30. When giving foot care you should soak the client feet for_____ minutes.

A. 15 to 20 minutes
B. 8 to 10 minutes
C. 2 to 3 minutes
D. 5 to 10 minutes

31. The following are needed when giving nail care except:

A. Orange stick
B. Hand towel
C. Kidney basin
D. Electric shavers

CIRCLE T IF THE STATEMENT IS TRUE AND F IF IT IS FALSE.

32. Razor blades are used to shave people who take anticoagulant drugs. T F

33. Feet are not easily infected without open wounds. T F

34. Brushing increases blood flow to one's scalp. T F

35. Nails are easier to trim after soaking or bathing. T F

36. Foot injuries are very serious for older people and those with circulatory disorders. T F

37. The loss of bladder control is called:

   A. Urinary urgency
   B. Urge incontinence
   C. Urinary Incontinence
   D. Stress incontinence

38. Another name for voiding is_____.

   A. Urination
   B. Dysuria
   C. Vomiting
   D. Nocturia

39. These substances increases urine production except:

   A. Coffee
   B. Cereals
   C. Tea
   D. Alcohol

40. Factors Affecting urine production are:

   A. Age
   B. Dietary salt
   C. Body temperature
   D. All of the above

41. Which of these is not a cause of urinary frequency?

   A. Trauma
   B. Bladder infection
   C. Pressure on the bladder
   D. Excess fluid intake

42. Causes of hematuria include the followings except:

   A. Kidney disease
   B. Shock
   C. Urinary tract infection
   D. Trauma

43. A tube used to drain or inject fluid through a body opening is called:

   A. Syringe
   B. Catheterization
   C. A catheter
   D. Micturition

44. A urinary catheter drains_____.

   A. Intestine
   B. Blood
   C. Feces
   D. Urine

45. Healthy adult produces about_____ ml (millimeters) of urine a day.

   A. 1200
   B. 1500
   C. 3000
   D. 500

46. You should not apply a condom catheter if the penis is_____.

   A. Long
   B. Red
   C. Firm
   D. Thick

47. The excessive formation of gases in the stomach and intestine is called:
   A. Flatus
   B. Fecal impaction
   C. Feces
   D. Flatulence

48. One of these is not a cause of fecal incontinence.

   A. Intestinal diseases
   B. Constipation
   C. Irritable bowel syndrome
   D. Nervous system diseases

49. Doctors order Enemas for the following reasons except:

   A. To remove feces
   B. To relieve constipation
   C. To increase blood circulation
   D. To clean the bowel off feces before certain surgeries and diagnostic procedures.

50. Enema tube is usually inserted___ to _____ inches in adults.

   A. 3 to 4
   B. 5 to 10
   C. 10 to 15
   D. 1 to 2

51. In what position should a client when receiving Enema?

    A. Prone position
    B. Fowler's position
    C. Supine position
    D. Lateral position

52. Which statement about the oil-retention Enema is incorrect?

    A. It relieves constipation and fecal impaction.
    B. Retaining oil hardens feces.
    C. It lets feces pass with ease.
    D. The oil is retained for 30 to 60 minutes

53. The purpose of a rectal tube is to:

    A. To gain control of bowel movement.
    B. To build up feces in the rectum.
    C. Relieve flatulence and intestinal distention
    D. To develop a regular pattern of elimination

54. Surgically Created Opening between the colon and abdominal wall is called:

    A. Colostomy
    B. An ostomy
    C. Ileostomy
    D. Peristalsis

55. Causes of diarrhea include the following except:

    A. Infections
    B. Irritating food
    C. Shock
    D. Microbes in food and water.

56. Which one is not a sign and symptom of dehydration?

    A. Flushed skin
    B. Soft Skin
    C. Coated tongue
    D. Oliguria

57. The backward flow of food from the stomach into the mouth is:

    A. Anorexia
    B. Regurgitation
    C. Enteral nutrition

D. Dehydration

58. A tube inserted through a surgically created opening into the stomach is called:

   A. Jejunostomy tube
   B. Nasointestinal tube
   C. Gastrostomy tube
   D. Nasogastric tube

59. The swelling of body tissues with is _____ .

   A. Enema
   B. Edema
   C. Dehydration
   D. Gauage

60. The amount of energy produced when the body burns food is called:

   A. A Calorie
   B. A nutrient
   C. Nutrition
   D. Dietary

61. Poor diet habits cause the following:

   A. Chronic illness to become worse
   B. Healing problems
   C. Increase the risk for acute and chronic diseases
   D. All of the above

62. Involuntary muscle contractions called _____ moves the food down the esophagus into the stomach.

   A. Peristalsis
   B. Pancreas movement
   C. Dysphagia
   D. Anus

63. One gram of fat produces _____ calories.

   A. 6
   B. 4
   C. 9
   D. 8

64. Which is a function of vitamin D?

A. Formation of red blood cell.
B. Absorption and metabolism of calcium and phosphorus.
C. Blood clotting
D. Muscle function

65. All are functions of vitamin C except (ascorbic acid) except:

   A. Nervous system function.
   B. Formation of substances that hold tissues together.
   C. Prevention of bleeding
   D. Wound healing

66. Sources of vitamin B_2 include the following except:

   A. Milk
   B. Liver
   C. Green leafy vegetables
   D. Pork

67. Which mineral allows red blood cells to carry oxygen?

   A. Potassium
   B. Iron
   C. Iodine
   D. Calcium

68. Which statement about carbohydrates is false?

   A. It provides energy and fiber for bowel movement.
   B. They are only found in breads.
   C. Carbohydrates breakdown into sugar during digestion.
   D. It provides the bulky part of chime for elimination.

69. Factors affecting nutrition and eating habits are:

   A. Age
   B. Culture
   C. Finances
   D. All of the above

70. Causes of anorexia involve the followings except:

   A. Rash
   B. Anxiety
   C. Pain
   D. Depression

71. Diabetes meal planning is for people with_____.
   A. Mental problem

B. Dementia

C. Diabetes mellitus

D. HIV

72. Diabetes is a chronic disease from lack of _____.

A. Vitamins

B. Water

C. Insulin

D. Sugar

73. If fluid intake exceeds fluid output, body tissues swell with water. This is called what?

A. Edema

B. Dehydration

C. Fluid Balance

D. Flow rate

74. A measuring container for fluid is called:

A. Gauage

B. Cylinder

C. Cone

D. Graduate

75. A graduate is used to measure the following except:

A. Left over fluids

B. Feces

C. Urine

D. Vomitus

76. Intravenous (IV) therapy means_____.

A. Use of foods and fluids by the body.

B. Amount of fluid taking in.

C. Fluids Guide pyramid

D. Giving fluids through a needle or catheter inserted into a vein.

77. The following norm requirements under OBRA promotes quality of life and comfort, rest and sleep, except:

A. Clean and orderly room

B. Room with more than 4 people

C. Room temperature between 71°F and 81°F

D. Adequate ventilation and room humidity

78. Which of the following is not a kind of pain?

A. Acute pain
B. Chronic pain
C. Insomnia pain
D. Radiating pain

79. Pain from a heart attack is often felt in the following areas except:

A. Left chest
B. Right groin
C. Left Arm
D. Left shoulder

80. Pain felt at the site of tissue damage and its nearby tissues is _____.

A. Radiating pain
B. Chronic pain
C. Phantom pain
D. Acute pain

81. Acute pain lasts for a short time and is usually less than _____ months.

A. Two
B. Ten
C. Six
D. Eight

82. Mr. Johnson was given a drug for pain, to protect him from injury. You should do the following except:

A. Raise the bed to the highest position
B. Provide help if he needs to get up
C. Raise bed rails as directed
D. Check on him every ten to fifteen minutes

83. Which words are not used to describe pain?

A. Cramping
B. Standing
C. Burning
D. Gnawing

84. Factors affecting reactions to pain include_____.

A. Past experience
B. Anxiety
C. Age
D. All of the above

85. Which one is a sign and symptom of pain?

    A. Low blood pressure
    B. Dry skin
    C. Nausea
    D. Cold

85. Relaxation means all except _____.

    A. To be calm, at ease and relaxed
    B. To be free from mental and physical stress
    C. A state of unconsciousness
    D. A state of well-being.

87. MR. Johnson has a blood transfusion going on. For the first one hour, his vital signs should be checked at least every:

    A. 25 minutes
    B. 5 minutes
    C. 15 minutes
    D. 30 minutes

88. Which one is not a nursing measure to promote comfort and relieve pain?

    A. Applying restraints
    B. Assisting with elimination needs
    C. Keeping bed linens tight and wrinkle free
    D. Positioning the person in good alignment

89. Circadian rhythm is a daily rhythm based on a _____ hour cycle.

    A. 6
    B. 10
    C. 12
    D. 24

90. The average sleep requirements for newborns (birth to 4 weeks) per day is:

    A. 11 to 12 hours per day
    B. 14 to 18 hours per day
    C. 12 to 14 hours per day
    D. 10 to 11 hours per day

91. A chronic condition in which the person cannot sleep or stay asleep all night is called_____.
    A. Distraction
    B. REM Sleep
    C. Insomnia
    D. Discomfort

92. Who orders bed rest?

    A. CNA
    B. Respiratory Therapist
    C. Doctor
    D. Occupational Therapist.

93. Bed rest is ordered for the following reasons except:

    A. Reduce pain
    B. Promote blood circulation
    C. Encourage rest
    D. Regain rest

94. Lack of joint mobility caused by abnormal shortening of muscle is _____.

    A. Contracture
    B. Atrophy
    C. Dislocation
    D. Syncope

95. Orthostatic hypotension means:

    A. Excessive straightening of a body part
    B. Brief Loss of consciousness
    C. Abnormal high blood pressure
    D. Abnormally low blood pressure when the person suddenly stands up.

96. Medical abbreviation for "range of motion" is:

    A. RFM
    B. ROM
    C. RUQ
    D. RPM

97. Another name for orthostatic hypotension is:

    A. Blood Hypotension
    B. Contractual hypotension
    C. Postural hypotension
    D. Syncope

98. Trochanter rolls helps to _____.
    A. Keep the hips abducted
    B. Prevent contractures of thumbs, fingers and wrist.
    C. Keep the weight of top linen off the feet and toes
    D. Keep the hips and legs from turning outward.

99. A trapeze is used for:

A. Exercises to strengthen arm muscles
B. Bending the foot down at the ankle.
C. Rotation of joint
D. Straightening of a body part

100. Range of motion exercise are usually done at least _____ times a day.

   A. 5
   B. 2
   C. 3
   D. 6

101. The PCT should record and report the following observations to the charge nurse when performing range of motion exercise to clients:

   A. Complaints of pain or signs of stiffness or spasm
   B. The time the exercise was performed
   C. The joint exercised
   D. All of the above

CIRCLE T IF THE STATEMENT IS TRUE AND F IF IT IS FALSE

102. Passive range of motion exercise is done by the patient. T F

103. Trapeze is also used to move-up and turn bed. T F

104. Adduction is moving a body part away from the midline of the body. T F

105. Exercise Helps prevents contractures, muscle atrophy. T F

106. Canes provide balance and support. T F

107. Four-point canes give more support than single-tip canes. T F

108. A cuff and measuring device used to measure blood pressure is called a…………

   A. Sphygmomanometer
   B. Stethoscope
   C. Adjustable value
   D. Manometer

109. The normal pulse rate for adult is _____ .

   A. 80-190 per minute
   B. 80-160 per minute
   C. 70-110 per minute
   D. 60-100 per minute

110. Which pulse rate is taking during CPR and other emergencies?

   A. Femoral
   B. Carotid
   C. Popliteal
   D. Brachial

111. Most often used pulse which is easy to reach and find is:
   A. Carotid
   B. Apical
   C. Radial
   D. Pedal

112. As a PCT which of the following set of vital signs should you report to the charge nurse immediately?

   A. T-99.6, P-82, R-16, BP-130/70
   B. T-98.6, P-65, R-18, BP-120/60
   C. T-97.6, P-81, R-20, BP-110/60
   D. T-105.5, P-100, R-40, BP-180/100

113. The pulse located in the neck is called:

   A. Carotid
   B. Temporal
   C. Brachial
   D. Femoral

114. The most accurate method of measuring body temperature is _____.

   A. Axial
   B. Oral
   C. Rectal
   D. Tympanic

115. The order "vital signs T.I.D" means to record vital signs:

   A. Every other day
   B. Three times a day
   C. Twice a day
   D. Four times a day

116. Which of these is a factor that does not increase pulse rate?

   A. Fear
   B. Anxiety
   C. Pain
   D. Sleep

117. Rectal temperatures are not taken if the person has the following except:

    A. Diabetes
    B. Diarrhea
    C. Rectal disorder or injury
    D. Confusion or is agitated

118. The amount of force needed to pump blood out of the heart into the arterial circulation is:

    A. Diastolic pressure
    B. Body temperature
    C. Systolic pressure
    D. Blood pressure

119. The PCT must use a stethoscope to determine the _____.

    A. Pedal pulse rate
    B. Apical pulse rate
    C. Femoral pulse rate
    D. Brachial pulse rate

CIRCLE T IF THE STATEMENT IS TRUE AND F IF IT IS FALSE.

120. Admission process starts at the admitting office. T F

121. Height and weight are measured on admission. T F

122. A patient is weighed while carrying her purse. T F

123. Transfer usually relates to change in condition. T F

124. The PCT can plan a client discharge. T F

125. If a person complains of pain, you should report it immediately. T F

126. Chairs and lift scales are used for people who cannot stand. T F

127. A digital scale should read at zero. T F

128. To measure weight gain or loss, the person should be weighed daily, weekly or monthly. T F

129. Before breakfast is the best time to weigh a person. T F

130. Food and fluids add weight. T F

131. Identifying information is obtained when the person arrives in the nursing unit. T F

132. You can use admission records to find a patient's personal data. T F

133. During admission procedure you will orient the person about the room, the nursing unit and the agency. T F

134. Admission to a nursing center or hospital causes anxiety and fear in patients. T F

135. A lighted instrument used to examine the external ear and the eardrum is called:
   A. Ophthalmoscope
   B. Telescope
   C. Oscilloscope
   D. Manometer

136. Which Of these is used to examine the inside of the nose?

   A. Laryngeal mirror
   B. Nasal speculum
   C. Ophthalmoscope
   D. Oscilloscope

137. Dorsal recumbent position is used to examine the following except:

   A. Abdomen
   B. Breasts
   C. Chest
   D. Spinal cord

138. The lithotomy position is used to examine what?

   A. Vagina
   B. Breast
   C. Rectum
   D. Heart

139. An Instrument used to open the Vagina so it and cervix can be examine is called:

   A. Nasal speculum
   B. Percussion Hammer
   C. Vaginal speculum
   D. Turning fork.

Section One Key	
1	C
2	C
3	D
4	B
5	A
6	A
7	D
8	C
9	C
10	B
11	A
12	A
13	B
14	C
15	D
16	B
17	D
18	D
19	A
20	B
21	C
22	B
23	D
24	C
25	B
26	D
27	C
28	B
29	C
30	B
31	D
32	C
33	C

34	D
35	B
36	D
37	A
38	C
39	D
40	A
41	B
42	C
43	B
44	D
45	A
46	C
47	A
48	C
49	B
50	C
51	A
52	B
53	D
54	B
55	C
56	A
57	B
58	C
59	C
60	C
61	C
62	A
63	C
64	B
65	C
66	D
67	D
68	B
69	A
70	C
71	C
72	A
73	A
74	D
75	B
76	C
77	B

78	D
79	A
80	B
81	C
82	B
83	A
84	B
85	D
86	A
87	D
88	C
89	A
90	D
91	A
92	B
93	C
94	A
95	C
96	B
97	A
98	D
99	B
100	B
101	C
102	B
103	B
104	A
105	D
106	D
107	A
108	D
109	D
110	C
111	D
112	B
113	C
114	B
115	C
116	A
117	A
118	C
119	C
120	A

SECTION TWO ANSWERS

1. D
2. C
3. B
4. A
5. D
6. C
7. B
8. A
9. C
10. D
11. C
12. B
13. A
14. D
15. C
16. B
17. A
18. B
19. D
20. C
21. B
22. D
23. C
24. B
25. T
26. T
27. T
28. F
29. F
30. T
31. T
32. T
33. T
34. F
35. T
36. C
37. D

38. B
39. C
40. A
41. B
42. D
43. A
44. C
45. D
46. B
47. C
48. B
49. B
50. D
51. A
52. D
53. B
54. B
55. B
56. D
57. A
58. C
59. A
60. D
61. B
62. C
63. C
64. B
65. A
66. D
67. B
68. C
69. C
70. B
71. D
72. A
73. C
74. D
75. C
76. B
77. A
78. C
79. D

80. B
81. C
82. D
83. A
84. C
85. D
86. C
87. D
88. A
89. C
90. D
91. B
92. C
93. C
94. A
95. B
96. C
97. D
98. C
99. B
100. A
101. D
102. B
103. A
104. C
105. D
106. B
107. D
108. D
109. A
110. D
111. B
112. B
113. C
114. A
115. D
116. B
117. A
118. B
119. C
120. A
121. C
122. D

123. C
124. B
125. A
126. C
127. B
128. A
129. C
130. B
131. D
132. C
133. B
134. A
135. C
136. B
137. D
138. B
139. A
140. C
141. D
142. B
143. C
144. A
145. B
146. C
147. A
148. D
149. B
150. D
151. B
152. A
153. D
154. C
155. B
156. A
157. C
158. B
159. D
160. C
161. B
162. A
163. D
164. B

165. C
166. B
167. B
168. A
169. C
170. B
171. B
172. A
173. B
174. D
175. C
176. T
177. T
178. F
179. F
180. T
181. C
182. B
183. D
184. C
185. B
186. A
187. D
188. B
189. C
190. A
191. B
192. D
193. C
194. B
195. T
196. F
197. T
198. F
199. T
200. T
201. C
202. B
203. A
204. B
205. C
206. D
207. A

208. B
209. D
210. B
211. C
212. A
213. B
214. D
215. C
216. C
217. C
218. B
219. A
220. D
221. B
222. A
223. D
224. C
225. A
226. C
227. B
228. D
229. B
230. B
231. D
232. A
233. C
234. B
235. D
236. C
237. A
238. B
239. D
240. C
241. C
242. B
243. D
244. A
245. C
246. B
247. B
248. A
249. C

250. C
251. B
252. C
253. D
254. B
255. C

Section Three key (EKG)	
1	B
2	B
3	D
4	A
5	A
6	C
7	D
8	D
9	B
10	B
11	A
12	B
13	B
14	A
15	C
16	B
17	C
18	D
19	A
20	C
21	C
22	D
23	B
24	B
25	B
26	C
27	B
28	C
29	C
30	B
31	D

32	D
33	A
34	C
35	D
36	C
37	B
38	A
39	C
40	A
41	D
42	C
43	A
44	A
45	C
46	D
47	D
48	A
49	A
50	D
51	B
52	B
53	A
54	C
55	A
56	D
57	A
58	B
59	A
60	C
61	A
62	A
63	D
64	D
65	B
66	A
67	D
68	B
69	A
70	B
71	D
72	B
73	A
74	B

75	C
76	D
77	C
78	D
79	C
80	C
81	B
82	C
83	A
84	A
85	A
86	B
87	B
88	C
89	D
90	D
91	C
92	C
93	A
94	A
95	D
96	B
97	B
98	C
99	C
100	D

ANSWERS TO SECTION FOUR

1C
2C
3A
4D
5B
6A
7D
8B
9C
10C
11A
12B
13A
14C

15D
16C
17B
18A
19A
20B
21B
22D
23B
24A
25A
26C
27D
28A
29C
30C
31C
32B
33A
34D
35B
36A
37B
38C
39A
40A
41A
42B
43D
44B
45A
46D
47C
48C
49B
50A
51A
52B
53D
54C
55B
56C
57D
58B
59A
60A
61C
62D
63B

64B
65A
66A
67B
68C
69C
70A
71A
72D
73C
74D
75C
76B
77C
78C
79A
80B
81D
82B
83C
84D
85D
86C
87C
88A
89C
90A
91C
92A
93B
94D
95A
96C
97C
98B
99A
100C

ANSWERS TO SECTION FIVE

1. B
2. C
3. A
4. A
5. D
6. A
7. D

8. C
9. B
10. C
11. D
12. C
13. B
14. D
15. C
16. D
17. B
18. C
19. C
20. B
21. A
22. D
23. C
24. B
25. C
26. D
27. B
28. C
29. A
30. A
31. D
32. B
33. D
34. A
35. C
36. B
37. A
38. D
39. B
40. C
41. D
42. B
43. A
44. D
45. C
46. C
47. A
48. B
49. D
50. F
51. F
52. T
53. T
54. T
55. T
56. T

57. F
58. T
59. T
60. T
61. T
62. F
63. T
64. T
65. A
66. D
67. C
68. B
69. D
70. C
71. A
72. C
73. A
74. B
75. C
76. A
77. B
78. C
79. A
80. F
81. T
82. T
83. T
84. T
85. F
86. T
87. T
88. T
89. T
90. C
91. A
92. C
93. A
94. D
95. B
96. D
97. B
98. A
99. C
100. C
101. D
102. A
103. C
104. B
105. C

106. A
107. B
108. D
109. A
110. B
111. C
112. A
113. D
114. B
115. D
116. A
117. B
118. D
119. A
120. D
121. C
122. B
123. C
124. A
125. D
126. B
127. C
128. T
129. T
130. T
131. F
132. T
133. T
134. T
135. A
136. C
137. B
138. D
139. A
140. C
141. B
142. A
143. C
144. B

ANSWERS FOR SECTION SIX
1. C
2. A
3. C
4. B
5. D
6. C
7. B
8. B

9. C
10. D
11. T
12. T
13. T
14. F
15. T
16. F
17. T
18. T
19. F
20. T
21. T
22. A
23. C
24. D
25. D
26. C
27. A
28. D
29. D
30. A
31. D
32. F
33. T
34. T
35. T
36. T
37. C
38. A
39. B
40. D
41. A
42. B
43. C
44. D
45. B
46. B
47. D
48. B
49. C
50. A
51. D
52. B
53. C
54. A
55. C
56. B
57. B

58. C
59. B
60. A
61. D
62. A
63. C
64. B
65. A
66. D
67. B
68. B
69. D
70. A
71. C
72. C
73. A
74. D
75. B
76. D
77. B
78. C
79. B
80. A
81. C
82. A
83. B
84. D
85. C
86. B
87. C
88. A
89. D
90. B
91. C
92. C
93. B
94. A
95. D
96. B
97. C
98. D
99. A
100. B
101. D
102. F
103. T
104. F
105. T
106. T

107. T
108. A
109. D
110. B
111. C
112. D
113. A
114. C
115. B
116. D
117. A
118. C
119. B
120. T
121. T
122. F
123. T
124. F
125. T
126. T
127. T
128. T
129. T
130. T
131. F
132. T
133. T
134. T
135. C
136. B
137. D
138. A
139. C

OTHER TITLES FROM THE SAME AUTHOR:

1. Director of Staff Development: The Nurse Educator
2. Crisis Prevention & Intervention in Healthcare: Management of Assaultive Behavior
3. CNA Exam Prep: Nurse Assistant Practice Test Questions. Vol. One
4. CNA Exam Prep: Nurse Assistant Practice Test Questions. Vol Two
5. IV Therapy & Blood Withdrawal Review Questions
6. Medical Assistant Test Preparation
7. EKG Test Prep
8. Phlebotomy Test Prep
9. The Home Health Aide Textbook
10. How to make a million in nursing

Order these books at www.bestamericanhealthed.com/resources.html
Or call 951 637 8332 for bulk purchase

Order these books at www.bestamericanhealthed.com/resources.html

Or call 951 637 8332 for bulk purchase

Made in the USA
San Bernardino, CA
04 January 2014